The Ultimate Sandwich Cookbook

Dishes, Volume 5

Olivia Bennett

Published by B&H Publishing Group, 2025.

THE ULTIMATE SANDWICH COOKBOOK

First edition. February 21, 2025.

Copyright © 2025 Olivia Bennett.

ISBN: 979-8230915928

Written by Olivia Bennett.

Table of Contents

To all the sandwich lovers, home cooks, and adventurous eaters who find joy in the simple pleasure of a well-crafted bite.

To my family and friends, whose laughter and shared meals have inspired so many of these recipes.

And to the countless chefs, bakers, and food artisans around the world who continue to push the boundaries of flavor—thank you for making every meal an experience worth savoring.

May your sandwiches always be delicious, your bread perfectly toasted, and your creativity endless.

Introduction: The Art of Sandwich-Making

Sandwiches hold a unique place in culinary culture, straddling the line between simplicity and sophistication. From the grab-and-go options that fuel our busy days to the elaborate constructions that grace fine dining menus, sandwiches are a universal favorite. They are versatile, portable, and endlessly customizable, making them the ultimate meal for any occasion.

In this chapter, we'll explore the fascinating history of the sandwich, break down the essential components of a great sandwich, and delve into why they've become a staple in cuisines worldwide.

The History of the Sandwich: From Humble Beginnings to Global Phenomenon

1. The Origin of the Name

The term "sandwich" is widely believed to have originated in 18th-century England, attributed to John Montagu, the 4th Earl of Sandwich. Legend has it that the Earl, an avid gambler, requested a meal he could eat without leaving the gaming table. His solution was simple: meat placed between two slices of bread, allowing him to eat with one hand while keeping the other free for cards. This innovation quickly gained popularity among his peers and was soon referred to as a "sandwich."

Pro Tip: While the Earl of Sandwich popularized the term, the concept of wrapping food in bread predates him by centuries.

2. Early Versions Around the World

Though the sandwich as we know it today was named in England, cultures around the globe had been creating similar dishes for centuries:

- Ancient Middle East: Flatbreads were used to scoop up meats and vegetables, much like modern wraps or pita sandwiches.

- Italy: The panini, grilled sandwiches filled with meats and cheeses, has its roots in Italian culinary traditions.

- China: Bao buns, though not technically sandwiches, share the same concept of enclosing savory fillings in a starchy exterior.

3. Evolution Through the Ages

As bread became more accessible and industrialized, sandwiches evolved from simple sustenance to a culinary art form:

- Industrial Revolution: Pre-sliced bread and processed meats made sandwiches a convenient lunch for workers.

- 20th Century: The invention of the grilled cheese sandwich and the rise of fast-food chains solidified the sandwich as an American staple.

- Modern Era: Artisanal breads, gourmet spreads, and global ingredients have elevated sandwiches into sophisticated creations.

The Components of a Great Sandwich

A truly great sandwich is more than the sum of its parts. It requires careful consideration of its components to achieve the perfect balance of flavor, texture, and presentation.

1. Bread: The Foundation

The bread is the canvas of your sandwich, and its type and quality can make or break the dish.

Types of Bread:

- Sliced Bread: Ideal for classic sandwiches like PB&J or BLT.

- Ciabatta and Focaccia: Perfect for hearty, rustic sandwiches.

- Bagels and English Muffins: Great for breakfast sandwiches.

- Wraps and Flatbreads: Excellent for portable, less messy options.

Pro Tip: Lightly toasting or grilling the bread enhances its flavor and prevents sogginess.

2. Fillings: The Star of the Show

The filling provides the primary flavors and textures of the sandwich. Common filling categories include:

- Proteins: Deli meats, grilled chicken, tofu, eggs, or seafood.
- Vegetables: Lettuce, tomatoes, cucumbers, or roasted veggies for texture and freshness.
- Cheeses: From sharp cheddar to creamy brie, cheese adds richness and depth.

Pro Tip: Layer fillings strategically—denser items like meats should go on the bottom, while delicate ingredients like lettuce should sit on top to maintain structure.

3. Spreads: The Unsung Heroes

Spreads add moisture, flavor, and sometimes an extra layer of texture to a sandwich.

- Mayonnaise and Aioli: Creamy options that pair well with almost any filling.
- Mustards: Ranging from sweet honey mustard to spicy Dijon.
- Specialty Spreads: Hummus, pesto, tapenade, or guacamole for unique flavors.

Pro Tip: Spread evenly to ensure every bite is flavorful and balanced.

4. Balance: The Key to Perfection

The best sandwiches achieve a harmony of flavors and textures:

- Flavor Balance: Combine salty, sweet, acidic, and umami elements.
- Texture Balance: Mix crunchy (toasted bread, pickles) with creamy (spreads, cheeses).
- Temperature Balance: Warm fillings paired with cold, crisp toppings add contrast.

Example: A turkey and cranberry sandwich balances savory turkey, sweet cranberry sauce, and crunchy lettuce for a delightful combination.

Why Sandwiches Are the Ultimate Versatile Meal

1. Portability

Few meals are as portable as a sandwich. Whether it's a wrapped burrito, a stacked club sandwich, or a pita pocket, sandwiches are designed to travel without spilling or requiring utensils.

Example: The muffuletta, a classic Italian sandwich, was specifically created to be a portable meal for dock workers in New Orleans.

2. Customizability

Sandwiches are a blank canvas for creativity:

- Dietary Preferences: From gluten-free wraps to vegan fillings, sandwiches cater to every diet.

- Flavor Profiles: Use global ingredients to create culturally inspired sandwiches, such as banh mi or falafel wraps.

- Meal Occasions: Sandwiches can be adapted for breakfast, lunch, dinner, or dessert.

Pro Tip: Experiment with leftovers—turkey from last night's dinner can become today's hearty sandwich.

3. Universality

Every culture has its version of a sandwich, making it a universal food:

- France: The croque monsieur, a rich ham and cheese sandwich topped with béchamel sauce.

- Mexico: The torta, a hearty sandwich filled with meats, beans, and salsas.

- Vietnam: The banh mi, a baguette sandwich layered with pickled vegetables, meats, and fresh herbs.

4. Economical and Practical

Sandwiches are a cost-effective way to create delicious meals:

- Budget-Friendly: Simple ingredients like bread, eggs, and vegetables can yield endless combinations.

- Minimal Equipment: No fancy tools or appliances are required—just a good knife and a toaster.

Pro Tip: Batch prep sandwich components like grilled chicken or roasted vegetables to save time during the week.

Conclusion: A Journey into the World of Sandwiches

The art of sandwich-making is about more than just assembling ingredients between slices of bread; it's about crafting a meal that satisfies, excites, and nourishes. As you embark on this journey through the world of sandwiches, remember that the possibilities are endless. From classic comfort foods to gourmet creations, there's a sandwich for every taste, occasion, and mood.

In the chapters ahead, you'll learn how to master breakfast sandwiches, explore global flavors, and create artisanal masterpieces. Along the way, you'll discover tips and techniques to elevate your sandwich game, inspiring you to think beyond the basics and embrace the full potential of this beloved meal. So grab your favorite bread, gather your fillings, and let's get started on creating sandwiches that are not only delicious but also unforgettable.

Chapter 1: Morning Classics

Breakfast sandwiches are the perfect way to start the day—portable, versatile, and packed with flavor. They bring together the essential elements of breakfast—eggs, meats, cheeses, and breads—into a single handheld package. Whether you're rushing out the door or enjoying a leisurely morning, classic breakfast sandwiches like bacon, egg, and cheese; sausage muffins; and smoked salmon bagels provide comfort and nourishment.

In this chapter, we'll explore the timeless appeal of these morning classics, guide you through their recipes, and share tips to make quick and easy breakfast sandwiches a staple in your routine.

Why Breakfast Sandwiches Are a Morning Staple

1. Portable and Convenient

Breakfast sandwiches are the ultimate grab-and-go meal. With everything neatly packed between two slices of bread or a bagel, they're easy to eat on the move or at your desk.

Example: The sausage muffin, popularized by fast-food chains, is designed for portability, making it a favorite for commuters.

2. Customizable for Any Taste

The versatility of breakfast sandwiches allows for endless variations:

- Swap bacon for turkey sausage or plant-based patties.

- Use different breads, such as English muffins, croissants, or even waffles.

- Add fresh vegetables, herbs, or spreads for unique flavor combinations.

Pro Tip: Always keep a variety of breads and proteins on hand to mix and match.

3. Balanced and Satisfying

A well-made breakfast sandwich offers a balance of protein, carbs, and fats, providing sustained energy throughout the morning.

Morning Classic Recipes

1. Bacon, Egg, and Cheese Sandwich

The bacon, egg, and cheese sandwich is a quintessential breakfast classic, combining smoky bacon, creamy eggs, and melted cheese on toasted bread.

Ingredients (Serves 1):

- 2 slices of bread (or a bagel, English muffin, or croissant)

- 2 slices of bacon

- 1 large egg

- 1 slice of cheddar cheese (or your preferred cheese)

- Butter or mayonnaise (optional, for spreading)

- Salt and pepper to taste

Instructions:

1. Cook the Bacon: In a skillet, cook the bacon over medium heat until crispy. Remove and place on a paper towel to drain.

2. Prepare the Egg: Crack the egg into the skillet, season with salt and pepper, and cook to your preferred doneness (sunny-side up, over-easy, or scrambled).

3. Toast the Bread: Lightly butter the bread and toast it in the skillet or a toaster.

4. Assemble the Sandwich: Place the bacon and egg on one slice of bread, top with cheese, and close with the other slice.

Pro Tip: For extra indulgence, spread a layer of garlic aioli or sriracha mayo on the bread.

2. Sausage Muffin

This breakfast favorite is simple yet satisfying, with a savory sausage patty, a perfectly cooked egg, and a slice of melted cheese nestled in a toasted English muffin.

Ingredients (Serves 1):

- 1 English muffin, split

- 1 sausage patty (homemade or store-bought)

- 1 large egg

- 1 slice of American cheese (or your choice of cheese)
- Butter or mayonnaise (optional)

Instructions:

1. Cook the Sausage: In a skillet, cook the sausage patty over medium heat until browned on both sides and fully cooked. Remove and set aside.

2. Prepare the Egg: Crack the egg into the skillet and cook until set. Use a circular mold (or a Mason jar lid) to create a round egg that fits perfectly in the muffin.

3. Toast the Muffin: Butter the English muffin halves and toast until golden.

4. Assemble: Layer the sausage, egg, and cheese on the bottom half of the muffin. Top with the other half.

Pro Tip: For a healthier version, use turkey sausage or plant-based patties and whole-grain muffins.

3. Smoked Salmon Bagel

Elegant yet effortless, the smoked salmon bagel combines the richness of cream cheese with the salty, smoky flavor of salmon and the freshness of capers and onions.

Ingredients (Serves 1):
- 1 bagel, split and toasted
- 2-3 slices of smoked salmon
- 2 tablespoons cream cheese
- 2-3 thin slices of red onion
- 1 teaspoon capers
- Fresh dill for garnish (optional)
- Lemon wedge for serving

Instructions:

1. Toast the Bagel: Toast the bagel halves until golden brown.

2. Spread Cream Cheese: Generously spread cream cheese on each half.

3. Assemble: Layer smoked salmon, red onion slices, and capers on one half. Garnish with fresh dill if desired.

4. Serve: Squeeze a wedge of lemon over the salmon just before eating.

Pro Tip: Add sliced avocado or cucumber for extra texture and freshness.

Tips for Quick and Easy Breakfast Sandwiches

1. Prep Ahead for Busy Mornings

- Make-Ahead Components: Cook bacon or sausage in batches and store in the fridge or freezer.

- Egg Prep: Use a muffin tin to bake multiple eggs at once for a week's worth of sandwiches.

- Assemble and Freeze: Prepare full sandwiches (minus fresh vegetables) and freeze them. Reheat in the oven or microwave as needed.

2. Choose the Right Tools

- Non-Stick Skillet: Ensures eggs and meats cook evenly and don't stick.

- Circular Egg Molds: Create perfectly shaped eggs for sandwiches.

- Toaster Oven: Ideal for toasting bread and reheating sandwiches.

3. Experiment with Ingredients

- Protein Swaps: Try turkey bacon, plant-based patties, or grilled tofu.

- Cheese Options: Explore Swiss, provolone, or even brie for gourmet flair.

- Bread Choices: Opt for croissants, flatbreads, or even waffles for unique textures.

4. Customize to Your Taste

Breakfast sandwiches are endlessly adaptable:

- Add fresh greens like spinach or arugula for a nutritional boost.

- Incorporate sauces like hot sauce, pesto, or sriracha mayo for added flavor.

- Experiment with herbs and spices, such as chives or smoked paprika.

Why Morning Classics Never Go Out of Style

The enduring appeal of breakfast sandwiches lies in their ability to combine comfort, convenience, and creativity. From the indulgence of bacon, egg, and cheese to the sophistication of a smoked salmon bagel, these classics remain beloved staples in kitchens worldwide. Their adaptability means there's always room for innovation, making them perfect for every palate and occasion.

In the chapters ahead, we'll explore sweet and savory breakfast options, healthy twists, and even global-inspired morning sandwiches. But first, embrace these timeless classics, and let them inspire your mornings with warmth, flavor, and satisfaction.

Chapter 2: Sweet and Savory Breakfast Sandwiches

Sweet and savory breakfast sandwiches represent the best of both worlds, combining indulgent flavors with satisfying textures to create a morning meal that's both comforting and exciting. These sandwiches are ideal for those who enjoy the balance of sugar and salt, the richness of spreads and cheeses, and the unique contrasts that arise when unexpected flavors come together. In this chapter, we'll explore three standout recipes—Nutella and banana panini, maple-glazed ham croissant, and peanut butter and jelly waffle sandwich—and delve into the art of balancing sweet and savory elements to craft the perfect morning bite.

Why Sweet and Savory Breakfast Sandwiches Work

1. A Symbiotic Flavor Relationship

Sweet and savory flavors are naturally complementary, as sweetness can enhance the depth of savory ingredients while salt can amplify the natural sweetness in a dish.

Example: Maple syrup drizzled over crispy bacon creates a harmonious blend that appeals to multiple taste receptors.

2. Textural Contrast

Sweet and savory breakfast sandwiches often combine different textures, such as the crispiness of toasted bread with the creaminess of spreads or the chewiness of meats with the softness of fruits.

3. Versatility Across Palates

These sandwiches are adaptable for a wide range of preferences. Whether you prefer bold, rich flavors or lighter, nuanced combinations, sweet and savory options cater to every palate.

Pro Tip: Adjust sweetness or saltiness in your recipes to suit individual tastes, such as reducing sugar for a less sweet finish.

Recipes: Sweet and Savory Morning Favorites

1. Nutella and Banana Panini

This decadent breakfast sandwich pairs the creamy hazelnut-chocolate spread with the natural sweetness of bananas, all toasted to perfection between slices of crusty bread. It's simple yet indulgent, perfect for mornings when you want a touch of luxury.

Ingredients (Serves 1):

- 2 slices of crusty bread (e.g., sourdough or ciabatta)

- 2 tablespoons Nutella

- 1 ripe banana, sliced

- Butter (for grilling)

Instructions:

1. Spread Nutella: Spread Nutella evenly on one side of each slice of bread.

2. Add Banana: Layer banana slices over the Nutella on one slice of bread.

3. Assemble: Close the sandwich with the second slice, Nutella side facing the banana.

4. Grill: Heat a pan or panini press over medium heat. Butter the outside of the bread lightly and grill until golden brown and crispy on both sides, about 3-4 minutes per side.

5. Serve: Slice diagonally and serve warm.

Pro Tip: Add a sprinkle of cinnamon or a pinch of sea salt for added depth.

2. Maple-Glazed Ham Croissant

This sandwich marries the buttery flakiness of a croissant with the savory richness of ham and the sweet complexity of maple syrup, creating a sophisticated yet approachable breakfast option.

Ingredients (Serves 1):

- 1 large croissant
- 2-3 slices of deli ham (or leftover baked ham)
- 1 slice of Swiss or Gruyère cheese
- 1 tablespoon maple syrup
- 1 teaspoon Dijon mustard

Instructions:

1. Prepare the Glaze: In a small bowl, mix maple syrup and Dijon mustard. Brush this glaze over the ham slices.

2. Assemble the Sandwich: Slice the croissant in half horizontally. Layer the ham and cheese on the bottom half.

3. Toast: Place the assembled sandwich on a baking sheet and bake in a preheated oven at 375°F (190°C) for 5-7 minutes, or until the cheese is melted and the croissant is warm.

4. Serve: Close the croissant and enjoy warm.

Pro Tip: Add a handful of arugula for a peppery contrast or a fried egg for extra indulgence.

3. Peanut Butter and Jelly Waffle Sandwich

This playful twist on a childhood classic uses waffles as the bread, adding texture and a nostalgic feel to a timeless combination of peanut butter and jelly.

Ingredients (Serves 1):

- 2 waffles (homemade or store-bought)
- 2 tablespoons peanut butter (smooth or chunky)
- 2 tablespoons jelly or jam (your choice of flavor)
- Optional toppings: sliced strawberries, bananas, or a drizzle of honey

Instructions:

1. Toast the Waffles: Lightly toast the waffles until crisp and golden.

2. Spread Peanut Butter: Spread peanut butter on one waffle.

3. Add Jelly: Spread jelly on the other waffle.

4. Assemble: Layer optional toppings like sliced strawberries or bananas on the peanut butter, then close the sandwich with the jelly-topped waffle.

5. Serve: Slice in half or quarters and serve warm.

Pro Tip: For extra crunch, sprinkle granola or crushed nuts over the peanut butter before assembling.

Balancing Sweet and Savory Flavors

1. Choose the Right Ingredients

The key to balancing sweet and savory flavors is pairing complementary ingredients:

- Sweet Components: Jams, syrups, fruits, or honey.
- Savory Components: Cheeses, meats, or eggs.
- Bridging Ingredients: Items like Nutella or peanut butter work as bridges, combining elements of both sweet and savory.

2. Play with Proportions

Adjust the ratio of sweet to savory based on your preferences:

- Sweeter Sandwich: Increase the amount of syrup, jam, or fruit.
- Savory Sandwich: Add more cheese, meat, or mustard.

Pro Tip: A touch of acidity, such as a squeeze of lemon or a dash of vinegar, can balance overly sweet flavors.

3. Add Textural Contrast

Texture enhances the eating experience, so aim for contrasts between creamy, crunchy, soft, and chewy elements.

Example: The crispiness of toasted waffles pairs beautifully with the creamy peanut butter and sticky jelly in the waffle sandwich.

Tips for Sweet and Savory Breakfast Success

1. Prep Ahead

- Slice fruits, portion spreads, and pre-cook proteins to save time.

- Freeze waffles or croissants for quick access.

2. Use Fresh Ingredients

High-quality ingredients elevate the simplest recipes. Choose ripe fruits, artisanal breads, and fresh meats whenever possible.

3. Experiment with Add-Ons

Enhance your sandwiches with creative additions:

- Spices: Cinnamon, nutmeg, or smoked paprika.

- Herbs: Fresh basil, thyme, or arugula.

- Toppings: Honey, nuts, or chocolate shavings.

Why Sweet and Savory Breakfast Sandwiches Are Irresistible

Sweet and savory breakfast sandwiches provide the perfect combination of comfort and innovation. They cater to those who crave a little adventure in their morning meal and those who find joy in the familiar. Whether you're savoring the indulgence of a Nutella and banana panini, the refined elegance of a maple-glazed ham croissant, or the playful nostalgia of a peanut butter and jelly waffle sandwich, these recipes are sure to delight.

By mastering these techniques and exploring new combinations, you'll discover that sweet and savory breakfast sandwiches are far more than just a morning indulgence—they're an opportunity to express creativity, explore flavors, and start the day on a delicious note. In the next chapter, we'll dive into healthy breakfast sandwich options, proving that indulgence and nutrition can go hand in hand.

Chapter 3: Healthy Start Sandwiches

Healthy breakfast sandwiches offer a perfect blend of flavor, nutrition, and convenience. They are a fantastic way to start your day with balanced energy, whether you're looking to incorporate more vegetables, reduce processed ingredients, or simply enjoy a lighter meal. In this chapter, we'll explore three standout recipes—avocado toast with egg, veggie-packed breakfast wraps, and Greek yogurt and fruit flatbread—that prove eating healthy doesn't have to compromise taste.

In addition to the recipes, we'll cover tips for enhancing the nutritional value of breakfast sandwiches, guiding you on how to create meals that are both satisfying and nourishing.

Why Choose Healthy Breakfast Sandwiches?

1. Balanced Nutrition

A good breakfast sandwich provides a mix of macronutrients:
- Proteins: Eggs, Greek yogurt, or plant-based alternatives for muscle repair and satiety.
- Carbohydrates: Whole-grain breads and wraps for sustained energy.
- Fats: Healthy fats from avocado, nuts, or seeds to support brain function.
Pro Tip: Aim for a balance of protein, carbs, and fats in every sandwich to fuel your morning effectively.

2. Versatility

Healthy breakfast sandwiches cater to a variety of dietary needs, including vegetarian, vegan, and gluten-free preferences.
- Swap regular bread for gluten-free options.
- Replace eggs with tofu or chickpea flour for a plant-based twist.

3. Portability

These sandwiches are ideal for busy mornings, offering a quick and nutritious option that you can eat on the go.

Recipes: Healthy Start Sandwiches

1. Avocado Toast with Egg

Avocado toast has become a symbol of modern, healthy breakfasts, and for good reason. Its creamy texture and rich flavor pair perfectly with a protein-packed egg, creating a satisfying and nutritious meal.

Ingredients (Serves 1):

- 1 slice of whole-grain or sourdough bread
- 1/2 ripe avocado
- 1 large egg (poached, fried, or scrambled)
- Salt and black pepper to taste
- Optional toppings: red pepper flakes, chia seeds, or microgreens

Instructions:

1. Toast the Bread: Lightly toast the bread until golden and crispy.

2. Prepare the Avocado: Mash the avocado with a fork and season with salt and pepper.

3. Cook the Egg: Cook the egg to your preference—poached, fried, or scrambled.

4. Assemble the Sandwich: Spread the mashed avocado on the toast, place the egg on top, and add any optional toppings.

Pro Tip: Add a drizzle of olive oil or a squeeze of lemon juice for extra flavor.

2. Veggie-Packed Breakfast Wrap

This colorful breakfast wrap is loaded with fresh vegetables, making it a great way to sneak in extra nutrients first thing in the morning.

Ingredients (Serves 1):

- 1 whole-grain tortilla or wrap
- 2 large eggs or 1/2 cup scrambled tofu
- 1/4 cup diced bell peppers (red, yellow, or green)
- 1/4 cup baby spinach or kale, chopped
- 1/4 cup shredded carrots
- 1 tablespoon hummus or avocado spread
- Salt and black pepper to taste

Instructions:

1. Cook the Eggs or Tofu: Scramble the eggs or tofu with a pinch of salt and pepper. Set aside.

2. Sauté the Vegetables: Lightly sauté the bell peppers, spinach, and carrots until tender.

3. Assemble the Wrap: Spread hummus or avocado on the tortilla. Layer the scrambled eggs or tofu and sautéed vegetables.

4. Roll and Serve: Roll the wrap tightly, slice in half, and serve warm.

Pro Tip: Add a sprinkle of feta cheese or nutritional yeast for an extra flavor boost.

3. Greek Yogurt and Fruit Flatbread

For those with a sweet tooth, this Greek yogurt and fruit flatbread offers a refreshing, protein-packed breakfast option that's both light and energizing.

Ingredients (Serves 1):

- 1 small whole-grain flatbread or naan
- 1/2 cup Greek yogurt (plain or lightly sweetened)
- 1/4 cup mixed berries (strawberries, blueberries, raspberries)
- 1 tablespoon granola or chopped nuts
- 1 teaspoon honey or maple syrup

Instructions:

1. Prepare the Flatbread: Warm the flatbread in a toaster or oven until soft.

2. Spread Yogurt: Spread a generous layer of Greek yogurt over the flatbread.

3. Add Toppings: Arrange the berries on top and sprinkle with granola or nuts.

4. Drizzle with Sweetener: Finish with a drizzle of honey or maple syrup.

Pro Tip: Add a sprinkle of chia or flax seeds for added fiber and omega-3s.

Tips for Adding Nutritional Value to Breakfast Sandwiches

1. Opt for Whole Grains

Choose whole-grain breads, wraps, or flatbreads to increase fiber intake and provide sustained energy.

2. Incorporate More Vegetables

Sneak vegetables into your sandwiches for added vitamins, minerals, and antioxidants.
    - Ideas: Spinach, arugula, roasted sweet potatoes, or grilled zucchini.

3. Use Healthy Fats

Replace processed spreads with nutrient-rich options like avocado, nut butters, or tahini.

4. Prioritize Protein

Protein keeps you full and energized throughout the morning.
    - Examples: Eggs, tofu, Greek yogurt, or lean meats.
    Pro Tip: Add plant-based proteins like hummus, beans, or lentils for variety.

5. Add Superfood Toppings

Sprinkle chia seeds, hemp hearts, or flaxseeds for a boost of omega-3 fatty acids and fiber.

6. Limit Added Sugars

For sweeter sandwiches, use natural sweeteners like honey, maple syrup, or fresh fruits instead of processed sugars.

Balancing Flavor and Nutrition

1. Sweet and Savory Harmony

Combine sweet and savory elements to keep your taste buds excited:
    - Pair avocado with a drizzle of honey.
    - Add a dash of cinnamon to savory eggs for a subtle sweet touch.

2. Play with Textures

Incorporate contrasting textures for a more enjoyable eating experience:
    - Crunchy granola or nuts with creamy yogurt.
    - Crisp vegetables with soft scrambled eggs.

3. Experiment with Spices and Herbs

Spices and herbs enhance flavor without adding calories:
    - Spices: Paprika, turmeric, cumin.
    - Herbs: Fresh basil, cilantro, or dill.

Why Healthy Start Sandwiches Are Essential

Healthy breakfast sandwiches prove that nutritious meals can be delicious, convenient, and versatile. By incorporating whole, fresh ingredients and focusing on balance, these sandwiches offer a fantastic way to energize your morning and nourish your body. Whether it's the creamy richness of avocado toast, the vibrant colors of a veggie-packed wrap, or the natural sweetness of Greek yogurt and fruit, these recipes are designed to inspire and sustain.

As you experiment with these ideas, remember that breakfast is your first opportunity to fuel your day with intention and care. The next chapter will delve into creative breakfast sandwiches for kids, ensuring that even the pickiest eaters start their day on a healthy and happy note.

Chapter 4: Timeless Classics

Classic sandwiches like the BLT, grilled cheese, and club sandwich have earned their place in the culinary canon. These timeless favorites are loved for their simplicity, versatility, and ability to satisfy cravings for comfort food. With just a few ingredients, these sandwiches transform into hearty, flavorful meals that evoke nostalgia while remaining relevant for modern palates.

In this chapter, we'll delve into the history and enduring appeal of these classics, provide detailed recipes for the traditional versions, and explore modern twists that bring these sandwiches into the 21st century.

Why Classic Sandwiches Are Timeless

1. Simplicity and Accessibility

Classic sandwiches are built on simple ingredients that are often pantry staples. Their uncomplicated nature makes them accessible to cooks of all skill levels.

Example: A BLT requires just five ingredients: bread, bacon, lettuce, tomato, and mayonnaise.

2. Comfort and Nostalgia

For many, these sandwiches are tied to fond memories of childhood lunches or cozy dinners. The familiar flavors and textures evoke a sense of comfort and warmth.

3. Versatility

While the base recipes are straightforward, classic sandwiches can be easily customized with new ingredients or techniques, allowing for endless variations to suit any taste or dietary preference.

Recipes: Timeless Classics

1. The BLT: Crisp, Juicy Perfection

The BLT is a masterclass in simplicity, balancing crispy bacon, fresh lettuce, and juicy tomatoes between slices of toasted bread. Its success lies in the quality of its ingredients and the perfect balance of flavors and textures.

Ingredients (Serves 1):

- 2 slices of sandwich bread (white, whole-grain, or sourdough)
- 4 strips of crispy bacon
- 2-3 slices of ripe tomato
- 2 leaves of crisp lettuce (e.g., romaine or iceberg)
- 1-2 tablespoons mayonnaise
- Salt and black pepper to taste

Instructions:

1. Cook the Bacon: Fry the bacon in a skillet over medium heat until crispy. Drain on paper towels.

2. Toast the Bread: Lightly toast the bread slices.

3. Assemble the Sandwich: Spread mayonnaise on both slices of bread. Layer bacon, lettuce, and tomato on one slice. Season the tomatoes with salt and pepper.

4. Serve: Close the sandwich with the second slice of bread, slice in half, and serve immediately.

Pro Tip: Use thick-cut bacon for a meatier bite, and add avocado slices for extra creaminess.

2. Grilled Cheese: Gooey and Golden

Few sandwiches are as universally adored as the grilled cheese. With its gooey melted cheese encased in golden, buttery bread, it's a celebration of comfort food at its finest.

Ingredients (Serves 1):

- 2 slices of white or sourdough bread
- 2-3 slices of cheese (e.g., cheddar, American, or mozzarella)
- 2 tablespoons unsalted butter

Instructions:

1. Butter the Bread: Spread butter on one side of each slice of bread.

2. Assemble the Sandwich: Place the cheese slices between the unbuttered sides of the bread.

3. Grill: Heat a skillet over medium heat. Place the sandwich in the skillet, buttered side down, and cook until golden brown, about 3-4 minutes. Flip and repeat on the other side.

4. Serve: Slice and serve warm, preferably with a bowl of tomato soup.

Pro Tip: Add caramelized onions, crispy bacon, or a spread of Dijon mustard for a gourmet twist.

3. The Club Sandwich: Layers of Flavor

The club sandwich is a triple-decker masterpiece that combines layers of turkey or chicken, bacon, lettuce, tomato, and mayonnaise for a hearty and satisfying meal.

Ingredients (Serves 1):
- 3 slices of toasted sandwich bread
- 3-4 slices of cooked turkey or chicken breast
- 2 strips of bacon, cooked
- 2-3 slices of tomato
- 2 leaves of lettuce
- 2 tablespoons mayonnaise
- Salt and black pepper to taste

Instructions:

1. Prepare the Ingredients: Cook the bacon until crispy and toast the bread slices.

2. Assemble the Layers:
- Spread mayonnaise on one side of each slice of toast.
- Layer lettuce, turkey or chicken, and tomato on the first slice.
- Add the second slice of toast, mayonnaise side up, and layer bacon, lettuce, and tomato.
- Top with the final slice of toast, mayonnaise side down.

3. Secure and Slice: Use toothpicks to secure the sandwich and slice it into quarters diagonally.

4. Serve: Arrange the quarters on a plate and serve with chips or a pickle.

Pro Tip: Substitute smoked salmon or roasted vegetables for a unique twist on the traditional club.

Modern Twists on Classic Sandwiches

1. BLT Variations

- California BLT: Add sliced avocado and use multigrain bread.
    - Spicy BLT: Spread chipotle mayo on the bread and add pickled jalapeños.
    - Vegetarian BLT: Replace bacon with crispy smoked tempeh or coconut bacon.

2. Grilled Cheese Reinvented

- Caprese Grilled Cheese: Add fresh mozzarella, basil, and tomato slices, and drizzle with balsamic glaze.
    - Truffle Grilled Cheese: Use truffle butter and Gruyère cheese for a decadent upgrade.
    - Breakfast Grilled Cheese: Include a fried egg and sausage patty for a hearty morning option.

3. Club Sandwich Innovations

- Mediterranean Club: Replace turkey with grilled chicken, add hummus, and use pita bread.
    - Seafood Club: Layer smoked salmon or crab meat with avocado and arugula.
    - Vegan Club: Use marinated tofu or tempeh, vegan mayo, and roasted red peppers.

Tips for Perfecting Classic Sandwiches

1. Prioritize Quality Ingredients

Classic sandwiches rely on the quality of their ingredients for success:

- Bread: Opt for freshly baked bread or artisanal loaves for better texture and flavor.
- Cheese: Choose cheeses that melt well, such as cheddar or Gruyère.
- Produce: Use ripe tomatoes and crisp lettuce for freshness.

2. Layer Strategically

- Prevent Sogginess: Place dry ingredients like lettuce or cheese next to the bread to shield it from wet ingredients like tomatoes or spreads.
- Balance Textures: Combine crunchy (lettuce, bacon) with soft (cheese, spreads) for an enjoyable bite.

3. Experiment with Cooking Techniques

- Toast Wisely: Toasting bread adds structure and enhances flavor.
- Grill Evenly: Use medium heat to ensure the bread crisps without burning while the filling warms through.

Why Classic Sandwiches Endure

Classic sandwiches endure because they strike a perfect balance between simplicity and satisfaction. They're approachable yet adaptable, comforting yet versatile. Whether you're savoring the smoky crunch of a BLT, the melty richness of a grilled cheese, or the layered complexity of a club sandwich, these recipes are timeless for a reason.

By mastering the traditional versions and experimenting with modern twists, you can elevate these staples into culinary works of art. As we move into the next chapter, we'll explore hearty favorites that build on the foundation of these classics, offering even more ways to enjoy the world of sandwiches.

Chapter 5: Hearty Favorites

Hearty sandwiches are more than just a meal—they're an experience. Packed with substantial fillings and bursting with flavor, they cater to those moments when you crave something satisfying and indulgent. Sandwiches like the Reuben, Philly cheesesteak, and meatball sub have become icons in their own right, celebrated for their bold flavors and ability to deliver comfort in every bite.

In this chapter, we'll explore the origins and recipes of these classic hearty sandwiches, along with techniques for building substantial, balanced, and delicious creations.

Why Hearty Sandwiches Are Beloved

1. Substantial and Satisfying

Hearty sandwiches are a complete meal in handheld form. They combine protein, carbs, and a variety of textures to create a dish that feels indulgent and filling.

Example: The Philly cheesesteak's combination of juicy beef, melted cheese, and a crusty roll is the epitome of satisfying comfort food.

2. Bold, Memorable Flavors

These sandwiches often feature strong, complementary flavors, such as the tanginess of sauerkraut in a Reuben or the savory richness of marinara sauce in a meatball sub.

3. Nostalgia and Tradition

Many hearty sandwiches are tied to cultural or regional traditions, making them a nostalgic favorite for many. Their histories add depth and authenticity to their appeal.

Recipes: Hearty Favorites

1. Reuben Sandwich

The Reuben is a classic deli sandwich that combines the savory, tangy, and creamy into one irresistible bite. Traditionally made with corned beef, Swiss cheese, sauerkraut, and Russian dressing, it's a perfect example of balance and boldness.

Ingredients (Serves 1):

- 2 slices of rye bread
- 4 ounces corned beef, thinly sliced
- 2 slices Swiss cheese
- 1/4 cup sauerkraut, drained
- 1-2 tablespoons Russian dressing or Thousand Island dressing
- Butter for grilling

Instructions:

1. Prepare the Bread: Butter one side of each slice of rye bread.

2. Layer the Ingredients: On the unbuttered side of one slice, layer corned beef, Swiss cheese, and sauerkraut. Spread Russian dressing on the other slice of bread and place it on top, buttered side out.

3. Grill the Sandwich: Heat a skillet over medium heat. Grill the sandwich until golden brown and crispy on both sides, and the cheese is melted (about 3-4 minutes per side).

4. Serve: Slice in half and serve warm.

Pro Tip: Use pastrami for a smoky twist, or substitute turkey for a leaner option.

2. Philly Cheesesteak

Hailing from Philadelphia, the Philly cheesesteak is a legendary sandwich made with thinly sliced beef, melted cheese, and sautéed onions, all served on a crusty roll. It's simple yet deeply satisfying.

Ingredients (Serves 1):

- 1 hoagie roll or sub roll
- 6 ounces ribeye steak, thinly sliced (partially freezing the steak makes slicing easier)

- 1/2 cup sautéed onions
- 2 slices of provolone cheese or 1/4 cup Cheez Whiz
- 1 tablespoon oil or butter
- Optional: sautéed peppers or mushrooms

Instructions:

1. Prepare the Roll: Slice the hoagie roll lengthwise but don't cut all the way through. Toast lightly if desired.

2. Cook the Steak: Heat oil or butter in a skillet over medium-high heat. Cook the thinly sliced steak until browned, about 2-3 minutes. Season with salt and pepper.

3. Add the Onions and Cheese: Reduce heat to low. Add sautéed onions and top with cheese. Cover with a lid for 1 minute to melt the cheese.

4. Assemble the Sandwich: Transfer the steak mixture to the hoagie roll and serve immediately.

Pro Tip: Experiment with different cheeses, such as white American or mozzarella, for variations on the classic.

3. Meatball Sub

The meatball sub is a comforting combination of juicy meatballs, rich marinara sauce, and gooey melted cheese, all served on a soft sub roll. It's a crowd-pleaser that never fails to deliver.

Ingredients (Serves 1):

- 1 sub roll
- 4-5 cooked meatballs (beef, pork, turkey, or plant-based)
- 1/2 cup marinara sauce
- 1/4 cup shredded mozzarella cheese or 2 slices provolone cheese
- Optional: grated Parmesan cheese and fresh basil for garnish

Instructions:

1. Prepare the Roll: Slice the sub roll lengthwise and toast lightly if desired.

2. Heat the Meatballs: Warm the meatballs in a saucepan with the marinara sauce over medium heat.

3. Assemble the Sub: Place the meatballs and sauce in the roll. Top with mozzarella or provolone cheese.

4. Melt the Cheese: Place the sandwich under a broiler for 1-2 minutes, until the cheese is melted and bubbly.

5. Serve: Garnish with Parmesan cheese and fresh basil if desired.

Pro Tip: Add sautéed onions or peppers for extra flavor and texture.

Techniques for Building Substantial and Satisfying Sandwiches

1. Choose the Right Bread

The bread is the backbone of a hearty sandwich. It must be sturdy enough to hold substantial fillings without falling apart.

- Examples: Hoagie rolls, baguettes, ciabatta, or thick-sliced rye.

2. Layer Strategically

Proper layering ensures that every bite is balanced:

- Place wetter ingredients, like sauces, between dry components to avoid soggy bread.

- Distribute proteins evenly for consistent flavor.

3. Balance Flavors and Textures

Hearty sandwiches should have a variety of flavors and textures:

- Combine savory proteins with tangy sauces or pickled vegetables.

- Include a mix of crunchy (toasted bread, raw veggies) and creamy (cheese, spreads).

4. Don't Skimp on the Filling

A hearty sandwich should be generously filled but not overloaded to the point of falling apart. Aim for a balance that's indulgent yet manageable to eat.

Modern Twists on Hearty Favorites

1. Reuben Variations

- Turkey Reuben: Use roasted turkey instead of corned beef.

- Vegan Reuben: Replace meat with marinated tempeh and use dairy-free cheese and dressing.

- Spicy Reuben: Add pickled jalapeños or a sriracha mayo spread.

2. Philly Cheesesteak Innovations

- Chicken Cheesesteak: Substitute chicken for beef.

- Vegetarian Cheesesteak: Use sautéed portobello mushrooms or jackfruit.

- BBQ Cheesesteak: Toss the meat with barbecue sauce for a smoky twist.

3. Meatball Sub Updates

- Spicy Meatball Sub: Add crushed red pepper flakes to the marinara sauce.

- Pesto Meatball Sub: Swap marinara for basil pesto and add fresh mozzarella.

- Plant-Based Meatball Sub: Use vegan meatballs and dairy-free cheese for a plant-based alternative.

Tips for Perfecting Hearty Sandwiches

1. Prep Ahead

Make components like meatballs, sauces, or sautéed onions in advance to save time.

2. Use High-Quality Ingredients

The flavors in hearty sandwiches rely heavily on the quality of their ingredients:

- Meats: Choose fresh cuts or deli-sliced options.

- Cheeses: Opt for high-quality, meltable cheeses.

- Sauces: Use homemade or high-quality store-bought options.

3. Serve Warm

Many hearty sandwiches, like the Philly cheesesteak or meatball sub, are best enjoyed warm. Toast or grill components to enhance their flavor and texture.

Why Hearty Sandwiches Are a Universal Favorite

Hearty sandwiches like the Reuben, Philly cheesesteak, and meatball sub are beloved for their ability to combine bold flavors, rich textures, and comforting warmth. These sandwiches are meals in themselves, satisfying even the heartiest of appetites. By mastering these classics and experimenting with modern twists, you can create substantial and satisfying sandwiches that cater to any craving.

In the next chapter, we'll explore kid-friendly sandwiches that are as fun to make as they are to eat, proving that sandwiches truly are for everyone.

Chapter 6: Kid-Friendly Sandwiches

Sandwiches are a go-to meal for kids, combining simplicity, versatility, and the opportunity for creative flair. Whether packing lunches, preparing after-school snacks, or planning family dinners, kid-friendly sandwiches provide a perfect canvas to please even the pickiest eaters. With the right approach, they can be healthy, fun, and full of flavor.

In this chapter, we'll explore three crowd-pleasing recipes—sloppy joes, grilled peanut butter and jelly, and mini slider sandwiches—and share tips to make sandwiches appealing and engaging for kids.

Why Sandwiches Are Perfect for Kids

1. Customizable for Any Taste

Kids have unique and ever-changing preferences. Sandwiches are endlessly adaptable, allowing you to experiment with fillings, spreads, and bread types to suit their tastes.

Example: A classic PB&J can be transformed with almond butter and fresh fruit for a twist on the original.

2. Easy to Handle and Eat

Sandwiches are perfectly portioned and easy for little hands to hold, making them a practical choice for young diners.

3. A Vehicle for Creativity

From cutting bread into fun shapes to creating colorful layers, sandwiches invite creativity, making meal preparation a fun activity for both kids and parents.

Recipes: Kid-Friendly Favorites

1. Sloppy Joes

Sloppy joes are a nostalgic favorite that combines savory ground meat in a tangy sauce, served on a soft bun. They're messy, fun, and packed with flavor.

Ingredients (Serves 4):
- 1 pound ground beef, turkey, or plant-based meat
- 1/2 cup diced onion
- 1/2 cup diced bell pepper (optional)
- 1 cup ketchup
- 2 tablespoons brown sugar
- 1 tablespoon Worcestershire sauce
- 1 teaspoon mustard
- 4 hamburger buns

Instructions:

1. Cook the Meat: In a skillet over medium heat, cook the ground meat until browned. Drain excess fat if needed.

2. Add Vegetables: Stir in the onion and bell pepper, cooking until softened.

3. Make the Sauce: Mix ketchup, brown sugar, Worcestershire sauce, and mustard in a bowl. Add to the skillet and stir to coat the meat. Simmer for 5-7 minutes.

4. Assemble the Sandwich: Spoon the mixture onto the bottom half of each bun, top with the other half, and serve warm.

Pro Tip: Use slider buns for smaller portions, perfect for little hands.

2. Grilled Peanut Butter and Jelly

A warm and gooey twist on the classic PB&J, this sandwich elevates a beloved favorite with a crispy, buttery exterior.

Ingredients (Serves 1):
- 2 slices of bread (white, whole wheat, or gluten-free)
- 2 tablespoons peanut butter (or any nut or seed butter)
- 2 tablespoons jelly or jam (any flavor)
- 1 tablespoon butter

Instructions:

1. Assemble the Sandwich: Spread peanut butter on one slice of bread and jelly on the other. Press the slices together.

2. Butter the Bread: Spread butter on the outside of each slice.

3. Grill: Heat a skillet over medium heat. Grill the sandwich until golden brown on both sides, about 2-3 minutes per side.

4. Serve: Let cool slightly, slice into halves or quarters, and serve warm.

Pro Tip: Add banana slices or a sprinkle of cinnamon for extra flavor.

3. Mini Slider Sandwiches

Mini sliders are perfect for kids, offering bite-sized fun with endless customization options. From burgers to chicken nuggets, these sandwiches cater to a variety of tastes.

Ingredients (Serves 4):

- 8 slider buns or small dinner rolls

- 4 small burger patties, chicken tenders, or plant-based patties

- 4 slices of cheese (optional)

- Lettuce, tomato slices, and condiments for topping

Instructions:

1. Cook the Protein: Grill or cook the patties or tenders until fully cooked. Add cheese slices in the last minute of cooking to melt.

2. Toast the Buns: Lightly toast the slider buns.

3. Assemble the Sliders: Place the cooked protein on the bottom bun, add lettuce, tomato, and condiments, and top with the upper bun.

4. Serve: Arrange the sliders on a platter and let kids customize with their favorite toppings.

Pro Tip: Use different proteins, like turkey burgers or fish fillets, to mix things up.

Tips for Making Sandwiches Fun and Appealing for Kids

1. Get Creative with Shapes

Cut sandwiches into fun shapes using cookie cutters or sandwich molds.

- Ideas: Hearts, stars, animals, or seasonal shapes.

Pro Tip: Save the trimmings to make breadcrumbs or croutons to reduce waste.

2. Add Colorful Ingredients

Incorporate colorful fruits, vegetables, and spreads to make sandwiches visually appealing.

- Examples: Bright red tomatoes, leafy green spinach, or purple cabbage.

Pro Tip: Use rainbow layering to create a visually stunning sandwich.

3. Let Kids Participate

Involve children in the sandwich-making process:

- Let them choose ingredients or assemble their sandwiches.
- Turn it into a fun activity, such as a DIY sandwich bar.

Pro Tip: Pre-portion toppings and spreads to make it easy for kids to customize.

4. Make It Bite-Sized

Kids love mini versions of their favorite foods. Use slider buns, wraps, or halved bread slices for kid-friendly portions.

5. Sneak in Nutrition

Incorporate healthy ingredients into sandwiches without compromising flavor:

- Add grated carrots or zucchini to sloppy joe meat.
- Use whole-grain bread or wraps.
- Swap mayo for hummus or avocado.

6. Serve with Fun Sides

Pair sandwiches with kid-friendly sides to create a balanced meal:

- Fresh fruit slices
- Veggie sticks with dip
- Mini bags of popcorn

Why Kid-Friendly Sandwiches Are a Hit

Kid-friendly sandwiches are more than just a meal—they're an opportunity to create memories, encourage creativity, and foster healthy eating habits. Whether it's the messy fun of sloppy joes, the nostalgia of a warm PB&J, or the customizable joy of mini sliders, these sandwiches are guaranteed to bring smiles to the table.

By involving kids in the process and tailoring sandwiches to their tastes, you can turn mealtime into a fun and engaging experience. In the next chapter, we'll dive into global-inspired sandwiches, exploring flavors and techniques from around the world that will broaden your culinary horizons.

Chapter 7: Mediterranean-Inspired Sandwiches

Mediterranean cuisine is celebrated for its vibrant flavors, fresh ingredients, and emphasis on wholesome eating. Mediterranean-inspired sandwiches, such as the falafel pita, shawarma wrap, and caprese sandwich, are excellent examples of how this culinary tradition transforms simple ingredients into mouthwatering meals. These sandwiches not only deliver on flavor but also offer a balance of textures and nutritional benefits, making them both delicious and satisfying.

In this chapter, we'll explore the recipes for these iconic sandwiches and discuss how fresh herbs, olives, and cheeses can elevate their flavor profiles.

Why Mediterranean Sandwiches Are Beloved

1. Fresh and Flavorful Ingredients

Mediterranean sandwiches rely on high-quality, fresh ingredients like ripe tomatoes, crisp greens, tangy olives, and creamy cheeses. These elements create a harmony of flavors that is both refreshing and indulgent.

2. Nutritional Balance

These sandwiches often feature whole grains, lean proteins, healthy fats, and a variety of vegetables, making them nutrient-rich and satisfying.

3. Culinary Versatility

Mediterranean-inspired sandwiches are versatile, offering endless opportunities for customization. Whether you prefer meat, plant-based proteins, or seafood, these sandwiches can be adapted to suit any taste.

Recipes: Mediterranean-Inspired Sandwiches

1. Falafel Pita

Falafel, a classic Middle Eastern dish, is made from ground chickpeas blended with herbs and spices, then fried or baked to perfection. Stuffed into a warm pita and paired with fresh vegetables and creamy tahini sauce, it's a flavorful and hearty sandwich.

Ingredients (Serves 4):
- 8 falafel balls (homemade or store-bought)
- 4 whole-wheat pita breads
- 1 cup shredded lettuce
- 1 cup diced tomatoes
- 1/2 cup thinly sliced red onion
- 1/2 cup cucumber slices
- 1/4 cup tahini sauce (or hummus)
- Fresh parsley for garnish

Instructions:

1. Prepare the Falafel: Cook falafel balls according to package instructions or fry/bake homemade falafel.

2. Warm the Pita: Heat the pita breads briefly in a skillet or oven.

3. Assemble the Pita: Cut each pita in half to form pockets. Stuff each pocket with lettuce, tomatoes, onions, cucumbers, and falafel balls.

4. Drizzle with Sauce: Add a generous drizzle of tahini sauce or hummus. Garnish with parsley and serve.

Pro Tip: Add pickled turnips or hot sauce for an extra burst of flavor.

2. Shawarma Wrap

Shawarma is a popular street food throughout the Mediterranean and Middle East, featuring marinated and roasted meat wrapped in flatbread. This sandwich is packed with spices and complemented by creamy yogurt sauce and crisp vegetables.

Ingredients (Serves 4):
- 1 pound chicken thighs or beef strips
- 4 large flatbreads or tortillas
- 1 cup shredded lettuce
- 1/2 cup diced tomatoes

- 1/2 cup thinly sliced cucumbers
- 1/4 cup red onion slices
- 1/2 cup yogurt-based garlic sauce (tzatziki or toum)

For the Marinade:
- 2 tablespoons olive oil
- 1 tablespoon lemon juice
- 2 teaspoons ground cumin
- 1 teaspoon paprika
- 1/2 teaspoon turmeric
- 1/2 teaspoon ground coriander
- 1/4 teaspoon cinnamon
- Salt and black pepper to taste

Instructions:

1. Marinate the Meat: Combine marinade ingredients in a bowl. Add the meat, coat evenly, and refrigerate for at least 1 hour.

2. Cook the Meat: Grill or pan-fry the marinated meat until fully cooked. Slice into strips if necessary.

3. Warm the Flatbread: Heat the flatbread in a skillet or oven.

4. Assemble the Wrap: Place lettuce, tomatoes, cucumbers, onions, and cooked meat in the center of each flatbread. Drizzle with yogurt sauce and wrap tightly.

5. Serve: Slice the wrap in half and serve warm.

Pro Tip: Add crumbled feta cheese or a sprinkle of sumac for added authenticity.

3. Caprese Sandwich

The Caprese sandwich is a simple yet elegant combination of ripe tomatoes, fresh mozzarella, and basil, drizzled with olive oil and balsamic glaze. Served on crusty bread, it's a celebration of Italian flavors.

Ingredients (Serves 2):
- 4 slices of ciabatta or baguette
- 1 large ripe tomato, sliced
- 8 ounces fresh mozzarella, sliced
- Fresh basil leaves

- 2 tablespoons extra-virgin olive oil
- 1 tablespoon balsamic glaze
- Salt and black pepper to taste

Instructions:

1. Prepare the Bread: Toast the ciabatta or baguette slices lightly.

2. Assemble the Sandwich: Layer tomato slices, mozzarella, and basil leaves on one slice of bread. Drizzle with olive oil and balsamic glaze, and season with salt and pepper.

3. Close and Serve: Top with the second slice of bread, slice in half, and serve immediately.

Pro Tip: Add prosciutto for a savory twist or arugula for a peppery kick.

Enhancing Mediterranean Flavors

1. Use Fresh Herbs

Herbs like parsley, cilantro, dill, and basil are essential in Mediterranean cuisine. They add brightness and depth to sandwiches.

Examples:
- Sprinkle chopped parsley on falafel pitas.
- Add fresh dill to yogurt sauces.

2. Incorporate Olives

Olives and olive-based spreads like tapenade bring a salty, umami-rich element to sandwiches.

Examples:
- Add sliced Kalamata olives to shawarma wraps.
- Spread olive tapenade on ciabatta for a Caprese sandwich upgrade.

3. Experiment with Cheeses

Mediterranean cheeses like feta, halloumi, and fresh mozzarella elevate sandwiches with their distinct flavors and textures.

Examples:
- Crumble feta over falafel pitas.

- Grill halloumi slices for a unique sandwich filling.

4. Use High-Quality Olive Oil

A drizzle of good olive oil enhances the flavors of Mediterranean sandwiches, adding richness and depth.

Pro Tip: Choose extra-virgin olive oil for its robust flavor and health benefits.

Tips for Perfect Mediterranean Sandwiches

1. Prioritize Freshness

The success of Mediterranean sandwiches lies in the quality of the ingredients. Use ripe tomatoes, crisp lettuce, and fresh herbs for the best results.

2. Balance Flavors

Mediterranean cuisine thrives on balance. Combine tangy elements (yogurt, lemon) with savory (meats, cheeses) and fresh (vegetables, herbs).

3. Embrace Texture

Incorporate contrasting textures, such as crunchy cucumbers with creamy sauces or crisp bread with tender fillings.

Why Mediterranean Sandwiches Are Irresistible

Mediterranean-inspired sandwiches are a feast for the senses, combining vibrant colors, bold flavors, and satisfying textures. Whether it's the spiced richness of a shawarma wrap, the wholesome heartiness of a falafel pita, or the elegant simplicity of a Caprese sandwich, these recipes offer something for every palate. By incorporating fresh herbs, olives, and cheeses, you can elevate these sandwiches into unforgettable meals.

As you experiment with these recipes, remember that the Mediterranean culinary tradition celebrates balance, freshness, and a love for good food. Let these sandwiches inspire your next meal and transport you to the sunny shores of the Mediterranean. In the next chapter, we'll journey further into global flavors with Asian-inspired sandwiches that showcase bold and exciting combinations.

Chapter 8: Asian-Style Sandwiches

Asian-inspired sandwiches represent a delightful fusion of bold flavors, vibrant textures, and diverse culinary traditions. From the tangy pickled vegetables and umami-rich meats of a Vietnamese bánh mì to the savory-sweet punch of a teriyaki chicken wrap or the tender, spicy-sweet balance of Korean bulgogi sliders, these sandwiches take the concept of a handheld meal to the next level.

This chapter delves into the recipes for these iconic Asian-style sandwiches and explores how incorporating bold sauces, fresh herbs, and unique ingredients can create unforgettable flavor experiences.

Why Asian-Style Sandwiches Stand Out

1. Bold Flavor Profiles

Asian-style sandwiches often feature a mix of salty, sweet, tangy, and spicy flavors, creating a multi-dimensional taste that is both exciting and satisfying.

Example: The combination of savory beef, tangy pickles, and fresh herbs in a bánh mì highlights the balance typical of Asian cuisine.

2. Unique Ingredients

Asian sandwiches incorporate ingredients like soy sauce, sesame oil, pickled vegetables, and chili pastes, which add depth and authenticity.

3. Versatile and Adaptable

These sandwiches can be easily customized to suit dietary preferences, whether you're using tofu instead of meat, gluten-free wraps, or dairy-free sauces.

Recipes: Asian-Style Sandwiches

1. Bánh Mì

A Vietnamese classic, the bánh mì combines French-inspired baguettes with traditional Vietnamese ingredients, such as pickled vegetables, fresh herbs, and seasoned proteins.

Ingredients (Serves 2):
- 2 small baguettes or sandwich rolls
- 1/2 pound pork belly, grilled chicken, or tofu (marinated and cooked)
- 1/2 cup pickled daikon and carrots (recipe below)
- 1/4 cup cucumber slices
- 2 tablespoons mayonnaise
- 1 teaspoon soy sauce or Maggi seasoning
- Fresh cilantro for garnish

For Pickled Vegetables:
- 1/2 cup julienned daikon
- 1/2 cup julienned carrots
- 1/4 cup rice vinegar
- 1/4 cup water
- 1 tablespoon sugar
- 1 teaspoon salt

Instructions:

1. Prepare the Pickles: Mix rice vinegar, water, sugar, and salt in a bowl. Add daikon and carrots, and let marinate for at least 30 minutes.

2. Cook the Protein: Marinate pork belly, chicken, or tofu in soy sauce, garlic, and a touch of honey. Grill or pan-fry until cooked.

3. Assemble the Bánh Mì:
- Slice the baguette in half and spread mayonnaise on both sides.
- Add cucumber slices, pickled vegetables, and cooked protein.
- Drizzle with soy sauce or Maggi seasoning, and garnish with fresh cilantro.

4. Serve: Close the sandwich and enjoy immediately.

Pro Tip: Add sliced jalapeños or sriracha for extra heat.

2. Teriyaki Chicken Wrap

This Japanese-inspired wrap is a blend of sweet and savory, featuring teriyaki-glazed chicken, fresh vegetables, and a soft wrap to tie it all together.

Ingredients (Serves 2):

- 2 large wraps or flatbreads
- 1/2 pound boneless chicken thighs or breasts, sliced
- 1/4 cup teriyaki sauce (store-bought or homemade)
- 1/2 cup shredded lettuce
- 1/4 cup thinly sliced red cabbage
- 1/4 cup grated carrots
- 1 tablespoon sesame seeds (optional)

For Homemade Teriyaki Sauce:

- 1/4 cup soy sauce
- 2 tablespoons honey or brown sugar
- 1 tablespoon mirin or rice vinegar
- 1 teaspoon grated ginger
- 1 teaspoon cornstarch mixed with 2 tablespoons water (for thickening)

Instructions:

1. Make the Sauce (if homemade): Combine soy sauce, honey, mirin, and ginger in a saucepan. Simmer for 5 minutes. Add the cornstarch slurry and cook until thickened.

2. Cook the Chicken: Heat a skillet over medium heat. Sear the chicken slices until golden brown, then pour in teriyaki sauce and simmer until fully cooked.

3. Assemble the Wrap:

- Lay the wrap flat and layer lettuce, cabbage, and carrots.
- Add the teriyaki chicken and sprinkle with sesame seeds.
- Fold and roll tightly.

4. Serve: Slice in half and enjoy warm or cold.

Pro Tip: Use grilled tofu or seitan for a vegetarian alternative.

3. Korean Bulgogi Sliders

Bulgogi, or Korean marinated beef, is a star ingredient in these sliders. Served on soft buns with spicy mayo and fresh greens, they're perfect for gatherings or quick meals.

Ingredients (Serves 4):

- 8 slider buns
- 1/2 pound thinly sliced ribeye or sirloin beef
- 1/4 cup Korean BBQ marinade (recipe below)
- 1/4 cup spicy mayo (mix mayonnaise with sriracha or gochujang)
- 1/2 cup mixed greens
- 1/4 cup thinly sliced red onions

For Korean BBQ Marinade:

- 1/4 cup soy sauce
- 1 tablespoon sesame oil
- 1 tablespoon sugar
- 1 teaspoon grated ginger
- 1 clove garlic, minced
- 1 tablespoon grated pear or apple

Instructions:

1. Marinate the Beef: Combine marinade ingredients in a bowl. Add beef and let marinate for at least 30 minutes.

2. Cook the Beef: Heat a skillet or grill over high heat. Cook the marinated beef in batches until browned and caramelized.

3. Assemble the Sliders:

- Spread spicy mayo on the bottom half of each slider bun.
- Add a layer of mixed greens, a few slices of beef, and red onion.
- Top with the other half of the bun.

4. Serve: Arrange on a platter and serve warm.

Pro Tip: Add a fried egg on top for a decadent twist.

Incorporating Bold Flavors and Sauces

1. The Role of Sauces

Sauces are the cornerstone of Asian-style sandwiches, providing depth and character.

- Examples: Teriyaki glaze, spicy mayo, or hoisin sauce.

Pro Tip: Use homemade sauces to control flavor intensity and sweetness levels.

2. Fresh Herbs and Vegetables

Asian sandwiches often include fresh herbs like cilantro, Thai basil, or mint, which add brightness and balance. Crunchy vegetables like cucumbers and pickled radishes provide texture.

3. Sweet and Savory Balance

Many Asian dishes balance sweetness and saltiness, which can be achieved by combining soy sauce, sugar, and tangy vinegar in marinades and sauces.

4. Heat and Spice

Spicy elements, such as chili paste, sriracha, or fresh jalapeños, bring excitement and complexity to Asian sandwiches.

Tips for Perfect Asian-Style Sandwiches

1. Choose the Right Bread

The bread should complement the fillings:
- Use crusty baguettes for bánh mì.
- Opt for soft slider buns for bulgogi sandwiches.
- Choose pliable wraps for teriyaki chicken.

2. Marinate Proteins

Marinating proteins like beef, chicken, or tofu enhances their flavor and tenderness.

3. Embrace Garnishes

Garnishes like sesame seeds, pickled vegetables, and fresh herbs elevate the presentation and flavor of sandwiches.

Why Asian-Style Sandwiches Are Irresistible

Asian-inspired sandwiches bring together the best of two worlds: the convenience of handheld meals and the bold, complex flavors of Asian cuisine. Whether it's the tangy freshness of a bánh mì, the sweet-savory punch of a teriyaki chicken wrap, or the indulgent decadence of Korean bulgogi sliders, these sandwiches offer something for everyone.

By experimenting with sauces, herbs, and unique ingredients, you can create unforgettable flavor combinations that elevate your sandwich game. In the next chapter, we'll explore Latin American-inspired sandwiches, diving into the rich, vibrant flavors of tortas, Cubanos, and arepas.

Chapter 9: Latin American Sandwiches

Latin American sandwiches are a vibrant representation of the region's rich culinary heritage, combining bold spices, fresh ingredients, and unique cooking techniques. Each sandwich tells a story of culture, tradition, and flavor, offering a delicious way to explore the diverse cuisines of Latin America. From the savory, pressed perfection of a Cubano to the layered textures of a torta and the versatility of arepa sandwiches, these creations deliver satisfaction with every bite.

In this chapter, we'll delve into the recipes for these iconic sandwiches, explore the key spices and ingredients that define Latin cuisine, and provide tips for recreating these flavorful dishes at home.

The Essence of Latin American Sandwiches

1. Bold Flavors

Latin American cuisine is known for its bold use of spices, tangy marinades, and fresh herbs. Sandwiches often incorporate elements like garlic, cumin, lime, and chili peppers for layers of flavor.

Example: The Cubano balances savory roast pork with the tanginess of pickles and mustard.

2. Variety and Versatility

Latin American sandwiches vary widely in ingredients and preparation techniques, reflecting the diverse cultures of the region.

Examples:
- Mexican Tortas: Hearty sandwiches filled with meats, cheeses, and salsas.
- Colombian and Venezuelan Arepas: Corn-based bread pockets stuffed with a variety of fillings.

3. Balance of Textures

From crispy bread to creamy spreads and tender meats, Latin American sandwiches often combine contrasting textures for a satisfying eating experience.

Recipes: Latin American Sandwich Favorites

1. Cubano (Cuban Sandwich)

The Cubano is a Cuban classic, combining layers of roasted pork, ham, Swiss cheese, pickles, and mustard, all pressed between slices of crispy Cuban bread.

Ingredients (Serves 2):

- 2 large pieces of Cuban bread (or substitute with a soft baguette)
- 4 ounces roasted pork (homemade or store-bought)
- 4 ounces sliced ham
- 4 slices Swiss cheese
- 2 tablespoons yellow mustard
- 4-6 dill pickle slices
- 2 tablespoons butter

Instructions:

1. Prepare the Bread: Slice the Cuban bread in half lengthwise. Spread mustard on both halves.

2. Assemble the Sandwich: Layer roasted pork, ham, Swiss cheese, and pickles on the bottom half of the bread. Close with the top half.

3. Press and Grill: Heat a skillet or sandwich press over medium heat. Butter the outside of the sandwich and grill, pressing down with a heavy pan or press, until the bread is crispy and the cheese is melted (about 3-4 minutes per side).

4. Serve: Slice diagonally and serve warm.

Pro Tip: For authentic flavor, marinate the pork in a mojo sauce made with garlic, citrus, and oregano before roasting.

2. Torta

A Mexican torta is a hearty sandwich filled with layers of protein, vegetables, and sauces, all served on a soft roll. It's highly customizable, with fillings ranging from breaded chicken (milanesa) to carnitas or vegetarian options.

Ingredients (Serves 2):
- 2 bolillo or telera rolls (substitute with ciabatta or French rolls)
- 1/2 pound protein of choice (grilled chicken, beef, or carnitas)
- 1/4 cup refried beans
- 2 slices of cheese (queso fresco or mozzarella)
- 1 avocado, sliced
- 1/4 cup shredded lettuce
- 1/4 cup sliced tomato
- 2 tablespoons pickled jalapeños
- 2 tablespoons mayonnaise
- Hot sauce or salsa (optional)

Instructions:

1. Prepare the Protein: Cook the protein (grill, fry, or sauté) and set aside.

2. Toast the Bread: Slice the rolls in half and toast lightly.

3. Assemble the Torta:

- Spread refried beans on one side of the bread and mayonnaise on the other.

- Layer protein, cheese, avocado, lettuce, tomato, and pickled jalapeños.

- Drizzle with hot sauce or salsa if desired.

4. Serve: Close the sandwich, press lightly, and serve immediately.

Pro Tip: Add a fried egg or crispy bacon for an indulgent twist.

3. Arepa Sandwich

Arepas are cornmeal-based flatbreads popular in Colombia and Venezuela. They are grilled or fried and then stuffed with a variety of fillings, from shredded beef to black beans and cheese.

Ingredients (Serves 4):
- 2 cups pre-cooked cornmeal (masa harina or arepa flour)
- 2 1/2 cups warm water
- 1/2 teaspoon salt
- 1 cup shredded beef, chicken, or black beans
- 1/2 cup grated cheese (queso fresco or mozzarella)
- Optional toppings: avocado slices, plantains, or hot sauce

Instructions:

1. Make the Arepas:

- In a bowl, mix cornmeal, water, and salt until a dough forms. Let rest for 5 minutes.

- Divide the dough into 8 portions and shape into flat, round discs about 1/2 inch thick.

2. Cook the Arepas:

- Heat a skillet or griddle over medium heat and cook the arepas until golden brown, about 5 minutes per side.

3. Prepare the Fillings: Heat the shredded protein or black beans and set aside.

4. Assemble the Sandwich: Slice each arepa open, leaving one side attached, and fill with your choice of protein, cheese, and toppings.

5. Serve: Enjoy warm with a side of salsa or avocado.

Pro Tip: Fry the arepas for a crispier texture or bake for a lighter option.

Exploring the Flavors of Latin Cuisine

1. Essential Spices and Seasonings

Latin cuisine relies on a rich array of spices and seasonings to create bold and distinctive flavors:

- Cumin: Adds earthiness to meats and beans.

- Oregano: Used in marinades and sauces for an herbal touch.

- Chili Powders: From smoky chipotle to mild ancho, chilies provide heat and complexity.

2. Signature Ingredients

Certain ingredients are staples in Latin American cooking and give these sandwiches their unique character:

- Avocado: Creamy and rich, often used in tortas and as a topping for arepas.

- Pickled Vegetables: Add tanginess and crunch to sandwiches like the Cubano.

- Queso Fresco: A mild, crumbly cheese used in tortas and arepas.

3. Unique Marinades and Sauces

Latin sandwiches often feature flavorful marinades and sauces:
- Mojo Sauce: A citrus-garlic marinade for pork or chicken.
- Salsa Verde: A tangy green sauce made with tomatillos and cilantro.
- Chimichurri: A parsley and garlic sauce perfect for beef sandwiches.

Tips for Perfect Latin American Sandwiches

1. Prioritize Freshness

Use fresh produce, herbs, and high-quality meats for the best flavors.

2. Layer Strategically

Balance textures and flavors by layering ingredients thoughtfully:
- Place creamy elements like avocado or cheese next to crunchy vegetables.
- Use pickled or tangy components to offset rich proteins.

3. Toast or Press

Many Latin sandwiches benefit from toasting or pressing to create crispy exteriors and melt cheeses.

Why Latin American Sandwiches Are Irresistible

Latin American sandwiches bring together bold flavors, satisfying textures, and cultural traditions in a handheld meal. Whether it's the perfectly pressed layers of a Cubano, the hearty versatility of a torta, or the customizable nature of arepas, these sandwiches offer something for every palate. By incorporating key spices, fresh ingredients, and authentic cooking techniques, you can recreate these classics in your own kitchen and experience the vibrant flavors of Latin America.

As we continue exploring global sandwiches, the next chapter will take you to Europe, delving into artisanal and traditional options that have stood the test of time.

Chapter 10: Elevated Ingredients

Gourmet and artisanal sandwiches take the concept of handheld meals to an entirely new level, combining luxurious ingredients and refined techniques to create unforgettable culinary experiences. Elevating your sandwich game requires more than just fancy components—it's about thoughtful preparation, impeccable balance, and a commitment to quality. In this chapter, we'll explore three standout recipes—lobster roll, prosciutto and fig panini, and steak sandwich with caramelized onions—that showcase the art of using elevated ingredients. Along the way, we'll also cover tips for sourcing high-quality ingredients and maximizing their potential in your creations.

The Appeal of Gourmet Sandwiches

1. Luxury in Every Bite

Gourmet sandwiches often feature premium ingredients such as fresh seafood, aged cheeses, and artisanal breads, transforming a humble dish into a sophisticated treat.

Example: A lobster roll combines the sweetness of fresh lobster with the richness of butter, all nestled in a soft roll.

2. A Balance of Sophistication and Comfort

While they include elevated ingredients, gourmet sandwiches maintain the comforting, familiar essence of traditional sandwiches, making them approachable yet indulgent.

3. Versatility for Any Occasion

These sandwiches can shine at elegant dinners, upscale brunches, or even as indulgent midday meals.

Recipes: Elevated Sandwiches

1. Lobster Roll

A quintessential New England dish, the lobster roll highlights the natural sweetness of fresh lobster meat, complemented by a buttery roll and light seasoning.

Ingredients (Serves 2):
- 1 pound cooked lobster meat, chopped
- 2 top-split hot dog buns or brioche rolls
- 2 tablespoons mayonnaise
- 1 tablespoon melted butter
- 1 teaspoon lemon juice
- 1 teaspoon chopped chives
- Salt and black pepper to taste

Instructions:

1. Prepare the Lobster: In a bowl, mix lobster meat with mayonnaise, lemon juice, and chives. Season with salt and pepper.

2. Toast the Rolls: Brush the outsides of the buns with melted butter and toast in a skillet until golden.

3. Assemble the Rolls: Fill each bun generously with the lobster mixture. Drizzle a bit more butter on top if desired.

4. Serve: Garnish with additional chives and serve immediately.

Pro Tip: For a Connecticut-style lobster roll, skip the mayonnaise and toss the lobster meat in warm melted butter before serving.

2. Prosciutto and Fig Panini

This Italian-inspired panini combines the saltiness of prosciutto with the sweetness of fig jam, enhanced by creamy goat cheese and crusty bread.

Ingredients (Serves 2):
- 4 slices of ciabatta or sourdough bread
- 4 slices prosciutto
- 2 tablespoons fig jam
- 2 ounces goat cheese, softened
- 1/2 cup arugula
- Butter for grilling

Instructions:

1. Prepare the Bread: Spread fig jam on one side of two slices of bread and goat cheese on the other.

2. Assemble the Panini: Layer prosciutto and arugula between the slices, creating two sandwiches.

3. Grill the Panini: Butter the outsides of the bread and grill in a panini press or skillet until golden brown and heated through, about 3-4 minutes per side.

4. Serve: Slice diagonally and serve warm.

Pro Tip: Add a drizzle of balsamic glaze for extra depth of flavor.

3. Steak Sandwich with Caramelized Onions

A steak sandwich is a hearty, luxurious meal, elevated by tender, juicy steak and sweet caramelized onions on crusty bread.

Ingredients (Serves 2):

- 1 pound ribeye or sirloin steak
- 1 large onion, thinly sliced
- 2 crusty baguettes or rolls
- 2 tablespoons butter
- 1 tablespoon olive oil
- 1/4 cup mayonnaise or aioli
- 1 teaspoon Dijon mustard
- Salt and black pepper to taste

Instructions:

1. Caramelize the Onions: Heat butter and olive oil in a skillet over medium heat. Add onions and cook, stirring occasionally, until golden brown and caramelized (about 20-25 minutes). Set aside.

2. Cook the Steak: Season steak with salt and pepper. Sear in a hot skillet until cooked to your desired doneness. Let rest for 5 minutes before slicing thinly.

3. Prepare the Bread: Toast the baguettes or rolls lightly. Spread mayonnaise and Dijon mustard on one side.

4. Assemble the Sandwich: Layer sliced steak and caramelized onions on the bread. Close the sandwich and slice in half.

5. Serve: Pair with a side of arugula salad or crispy fries.

Pro Tip: Add slices of aged cheddar or Gruyère for extra indulgence.

Tips for Sourcing High-Quality Ingredients

1. Seafood

- Freshness is Key: Always use fresh, sustainably sourced seafood. Look for lobster or shrimp that smells clean and has a firm texture.

- Local Markets: Visit fish markets or specialty stores for the best selection.

2. Meats

- Choose the Right Cut: For steak sandwiches, ribeye, striploin, or sirloin are excellent choices for their tenderness and flavor.

- Dry-Aged Beef: Opt for dry-aged cuts when possible for enhanced flavor.

3. Bread

- Artisanal Breads: Use freshly baked bread with a sturdy crust and soft interior, such as ciabatta, sourdough, or baguettes.

- Specialty Options: For added variety, try brioche rolls, focaccia, or seeded loaves.

4. Cheeses

- Aged and Artisanal: Use high-quality cheeses like aged cheddar, Gruyère, or creamy goat cheese to elevate the flavor profile.

- Storage Tips: Store cheese in parchment paper in the refrigerator to maintain freshness.

5. Produce

- Fresh and Seasonal: Incorporate ripe, seasonal fruits and vegetables for the best flavor and nutritional value.

- Local and Organic: Shop at farmers' markets or organic stores for superior quality.

6. Specialty Ingredients

- Unique Additions: Items like fig jam, balsamic glaze, and truffle butter can elevate your sandwiches to gourmet levels.

- Where to Buy: Check specialty food stores or online retailers for hard-to-find items.

Why Elevated Ingredients Make a Difference

1. Flavor and Texture

High-quality ingredients provide depth of flavor and improved textures, resulting in a more enjoyable eating experience.

2. Presentation

Premium ingredients elevate the visual appeal of your sandwiches, making them look as good as they taste.

3. Culinary Confidence

Using elevated ingredients encourages creativity and fosters confidence in the kitchen, allowing you to experiment with new combinations and techniques.

Crafting Gourmet Sandwiches: Final Thoughts

Gourmet sandwiches are more than just meals—they are culinary masterpieces that celebrate the art of combining elevated ingredients. Whether indulging in the luxurious sweetness of a lobster roll, the harmonious balance of a prosciutto and fig panini, or the robust flavors of a steak sandwich with caramelized onions, these recipes highlight the transformative power of high-quality components.

By sourcing the best ingredients, paying attention to detail, and experimenting with flavors, you can create sandwiches that delight and impress. In the next chapter, we'll explore vegetarian and vegan gourmet options, proving that plant-based sandwiches can be just as indulgent and satisfying as their meat-filled counterparts.

Chapter 11: Vegetarian and Vegan Gourmet Options

Vegetarian and vegan gourmet sandwiches showcase the creativity and versatility of plant-based cuisine. With the right combination of flavors, textures, and high-quality ingredients, these sandwiches can rival their meat-filled counterparts, offering satisfaction and indulgence in every bite. From the hearty flavors of roasted vegetable focaccia to the creamy richness of avocado and chickpea mash, and the gooey delight of vegan grilled cheese, plant-based sandwiches can be as gourmet as they are delicious.

In this chapter, we'll explore these three standout recipes, provide tips for making vegetarian and vegan sandwiches flavorful and satisfying, and discuss how to create balance and depth using plant-based ingredients.

Why Vegetarian and Vegan Sandwiches Are Rising in Popularity

1. Health and Wellness Benefits

Plant-based diets are associated with numerous health benefits, including improved heart health, reduced inflammation, and better digestion. Sandwiches that emphasize whole, plant-based ingredients are a convenient and delicious way to incorporate more vegetables, legumes, and whole grains into your diet.

2. Environmental Impact

Choosing plant-based meals reduces your carbon footprint, making it a sustainable option for eco-conscious eaters.

3. Culinary Creativity

Vegetarian and vegan sandwiches encourage experimentation with bold flavors, unique ingredients, and innovative techniques.

Recipes: Vegetarian and Vegan Gourmet Sandwiches

1. Roasted Vegetable Focaccia

This hearty, Italian-inspired sandwich features a medley of roasted vegetables layered on soft, herbaceous focaccia bread. The combination of caramelized flavors, creamy spreads, and fresh greens makes it a satisfying meal.

Ingredients (Serves 2):

- 1 loaf focaccia bread, sliced horizontally

- 1 cup mixed roasted vegetables (zucchini, bell peppers, eggplant, and mushrooms)

- 1/4 cup hummus or basil pesto (vegan if preferred)

- 1/2 cup fresh arugula or spinach

- 1 tablespoon balsamic glaze

- Salt and black pepper to taste

Instructions:

1. Roast the Vegetables:

- Preheat the oven to 400°F (200°C).

- Toss sliced vegetables with olive oil, salt, and pepper. Spread them on a baking sheet and roast for 20-25 minutes, flipping halfway through, until tender and caramelized.

2. Prepare the Focaccia:

- Slice the focaccia horizontally and toast lightly if desired. Spread hummus or pesto on the bottom half.

3. Assemble the Sandwich:

- Layer roasted vegetables evenly on the bread.

- Add fresh arugula and drizzle with balsamic glaze.

- Close the sandwich with the top half of the focaccia.

4. Serve: Slice into portions and enjoy warm or at room temperature.

Pro Tip: Add marinated artichoke hearts or sun-dried tomatoes for extra flavor.

2. Avocado and Chickpea Mash Sandwich

This creamy, protein-packed sandwich pairs the buttery richness of avocado with the satisfying texture of chickpeas, all enhanced with fresh herbs and spices.

Ingredients (Serves 2):

- 4 slices of whole-grain bread or sourdough
- 1 ripe avocado
- 1/2 cup cooked chickpeas (canned or freshly cooked)
- 1 tablespoon lemon juice
- 1/2 teaspoon garlic powder
- 1/4 teaspoon smoked paprika (optional)
- Salt and black pepper to taste
- Optional toppings: sliced tomatoes, cucumber, or microgreens

Instructions:

1. Prepare the Mash:

- In a bowl, mash the avocado and chickpeas together with a fork until combined but slightly chunky.

- Stir in lemon juice, garlic powder, smoked paprika, salt, and pepper.

2. Toast the Bread: Lightly toast the bread slices for added texture.

3. Assemble the Sandwich:

- Spread the avocado and chickpea mash on one slice of bread.

- Add optional toppings like sliced tomatoes or cucumber for extra freshness.

- Close the sandwich with the second slice of bread.

4. Serve: Slice diagonally and serve immediately.

Pro Tip: For a Mediterranean twist, add crumbled vegan feta or a drizzle of tahini.

3. Vegan Grilled Cheese

A plant-based take on the classic comfort food, this vegan grilled cheese combines melty dairy-free cheese with caramelized onions and a hint of garlic for an elevated twist.

Ingredients (Serves 2):

- 4 slices of crusty bread (sourdough or multigrain)
- 4 slices of vegan cheese (cheddar, mozzarella, or a blend)
- 1 small onion, thinly sliced

- 2 tablespoons vegan butter

- 1 teaspoon garlic powder

Instructions:

1. Caramelize the Onions:

- Heat 1 tablespoon of vegan butter in a skillet over medium heat. Add onions and cook, stirring occasionally, until caramelized (10-15 minutes). Set aside.

2. Prepare the Bread:

- Butter one side of each slice of bread and sprinkle with garlic powder.

3. Assemble the Sandwich:

- Place two slices of bread, buttered side down, in the skillet.

- Layer vegan cheese and caramelized onions on top. Close with the remaining slices of bread, buttered side up.

4. Grill the Sandwich:

- Cook over medium heat until golden brown on both sides and the cheese is melted, about 3-4 minutes per side.

5. Serve: Slice and serve warm.

Pro Tip: Add fresh spinach or sautéed mushrooms for extra layers of flavor.

Making Plant-Based Sandwiches Satisfying and Flavorful

1. Layer Flavors Thoughtfully

Combine ingredients that balance and complement each other:

- Savory: Use umami-rich elements like mushrooms, sun-dried tomatoes, or nutritional yeast.

- Tangy: Add a splash of lemon juice, balsamic glaze, or pickled vegetables.

- Creamy: Incorporate avocado, hummus, or plant-based cheeses.

2. Experiment with Textures

Create contrast with a mix of soft, crunchy, and chewy elements:

- Soft: Mashed chickpeas, roasted vegetables, or vegan cheeses.

- Crunchy: Toasted bread, fresh greens, or nuts.

3. Use High-Quality Ingredients

- Opt for fresh, seasonal produce for vibrant flavors.
    - Choose artisanal bread for a sturdy and flavorful base.

4. Incorporate Herbs and Spices

Fresh herbs like cilantro, parsley, and basil add brightness, while spices like smoked paprika, cumin, and turmeric enhance depth.

The Appeal of Plant-Based Gourmet Sandwiches

1. Healthy and Nutritious
    Packed with vegetables, legumes, and whole grains, these sandwiches offer a nutrient-dense alternative to traditional options.

2. Environmentally Friendly
    Plant-based eating supports sustainability, making these sandwiches a responsible choice for the planet.
    3. Innovative and Delicious
    Plant-based sandwiches prove that gourmet meals don't need meat or dairy to be indulgent, flavorful, and satisfying.

Final Thoughts: Plant-Based Sandwich Creativity

Vegetarian and vegan gourmet sandwiches are a celebration of innovation, flavor, and wholesome ingredients. Whether you're savoring the smoky depth of roasted vegetable focaccia, the creamy richness of avocado and chickpea mash, or the gooey delight of vegan grilled cheese, these recipes highlight the potential of plant-based cuisine.

By experimenting with textures, flavors, and high-quality ingredients, you can create sandwiches that are not only satisfying but also showcase the artistry of vegetarian and vegan cooking. In the next chapter, we'll explore the sweet side of gourmet sandwiches with decadent dessert-inspired creations.

Chapter 12: Sweet and Dessert Sandwiches

Sweet and dessert sandwiches offer a delightful twist on the traditional sandwich, transforming everyday ingredients into indulgent treats. These creations are not only perfect for satisfying your sweet tooth but also provide an opportunity to experiment with flavors, textures, and presentation. Whether you're crafting a nostalgic ice cream sandwich, a gooey s'mores panini, or an elegant mascarpone and berry toast, sweet sandwiches are a versatile way to celebrate dessert in handheld form.

In this chapter, we'll explore recipes for these decadent sandwiches, provide techniques for crafting indulgent creations, and offer tips for balancing sweetness with complementary flavors.

Why Sweet Sandwiches Are Unique

1. A Creative Culinary Experience

Sweet sandwiches allow for endless creativity by combining unexpected ingredients to produce new flavors and textures.

Example: A mascarpone and berry toast balances creamy, tart, and sweet elements for a sophisticated treat.

2. Versatile and Customizable

These sandwiches can be tailored to suit different tastes and occasions, from kid-friendly ice cream sandwiches to elegant desserts for dinner parties.

3. Portable Indulgence

Sweet sandwiches are inherently portable, making them perfect for picnics, parties, or as an easy dessert option.

Recipes: Sweet and Dessert Sandwich Favorites

1. Ice Cream Sandwich

The ultimate nostalgic treat, the ice cream sandwich combines creamy, cold ice cream with soft cookies or crisp wafers for a dessert that's both refreshing and indulgent.

Ingredients (Makes 6 sandwiches):

- 12 cookies (chocolate chip, sugar, or brownie cookies)

- 3 cups ice cream (vanilla, chocolate, or your preferred flavor)

- Optional: sprinkles, crushed nuts, or mini chocolate chips for rolling

Instructions:

1. Soften the Ice Cream: Let the ice cream sit at room temperature for 5-10 minutes until slightly softened but not melted.

2. Assemble the Sandwiches:

- Place a scoop of ice cream on the flat side of one cookie.

- Top with another cookie, flat side down, and press gently to spread the ice cream evenly.

3. Decorate (Optional): Roll the edges of the ice cream in sprinkles, crushed nuts, or mini chocolate chips.

4. Freeze: Place the assembled sandwiches on a baking sheet and freeze for 1 hour to firm up.

5. Serve: Enjoy straight from the freezer or wrap individually for later.

Pro Tip: Use homemade cookies for a personalized touch and experiment with unique ice cream flavors like salted caramel or mint chocolate chip.

2. S'mores Panini

A grown-up take on the campfire classic, the s'mores panini layers gooey marshmallows, melted chocolate, and graham cracker crumbs between slices of buttery, grilled bread.

Ingredients (Serves 2):

- 4 slices of bread (brioche or white sandwich bread)

- 1/2 cup mini marshmallows or marshmallow fluff

- 2 ounces milk or dark chocolate, chopped

- 2 tablespoons graham cracker crumbs

- 2 tablespoons butter

Instructions:

1. Prepare the Bread: Butter one side of each slice of bread.

2. Assemble the Panini:

- Place marshmallows or marshmallow fluff on the unbuttered side of two slices.

- Sprinkle with chopped chocolate and graham cracker crumbs.

- Top with the remaining slices of bread, buttered side out.

3. Grill the Panini: Heat a panini press or skillet over medium heat. Grill the sandwiches until golden brown and the filling is melted, about 3-4 minutes per side.

4. Serve: Slice and serve warm for maximum gooeyness.

Pro Tip: Add a pinch of sea salt to the chocolate for a sophisticated flavor boost.

3. Mascarpone and Berry Toast

This elegant dessert sandwich combines creamy mascarpone cheese with fresh berries and a drizzle of honey, all served on crisp, toasted bread.

Ingredients (Serves 2):

- 4 slices of brioche or sourdough bread

- 1/2 cup mascarpone cheese, softened

- 1 cup mixed fresh berries (strawberries, blueberries, raspberries)

- 2 tablespoons honey or maple syrup

- Optional: mint leaves or powdered sugar for garnish

Instructions:

1. Prepare the Bread: Toast the slices of bread until golden brown.

2. Spread the Mascarpone: Spread a generous layer of mascarpone cheese on each slice.

3. Add the Berries: Top with mixed berries, arranging them evenly across the surface.

4. Drizzle and Garnish: Drizzle with honey or maple syrup and garnish with mint leaves or a dusting of powdered sugar.

5. Serve: Enjoy immediately as a light dessert or afternoon treat.

Pro Tip: Use seasonal fruits for the freshest flavor, or swap mascarpone for ricotta for a slightly different texture.

Techniques for Crafting Indulgent Sweet Sandwiches

1. Balance Sweetness
   Avoid overwhelming sweetness by incorporating contrasting flavors:
   - Add a hint of salt to caramel or chocolate components.
   - Use tart fruits like raspberries or citrus to offset richness.
   2. Play with Textures
   Combine soft, creamy, and crunchy elements for a multi-dimensional eating experience:
   - Soft: Ice cream or mascarpone cheese.
   - Crunchy: Cookies, graham cracker crumbs, or toasted bread.
   3. Use High-Quality Ingredients
   The success of dessert sandwiches depends on the quality of their components:
   - Chocolate: Use premium chocolate for deeper flavor.
   - Fruit: Choose ripe, fresh fruit for maximum sweetness and juiciness.
   4. Experiment with Bread Options
   Bread is the foundation of a sweet sandwich, so choose wisely:
   - Soft and Rich: Brioche, challah, or Hawaiian rolls.
   - Crunchy and Light: Toasted sourdough or waffle slices.

Ideas for Customizing Sweet Sandwiches

1. Ice Cream Sandwich Variations
   - Flavorful Additions: Incorporate swirls of caramel, peanut butter, or fruit compotes in the ice cream.
   - Unique Coatings: Roll the edges in crushed pretzels, freeze-dried fruit, or coconut flakes.
   2. S'mores Panini Twists
   - Nutty Delight: Spread hazelnut or almond butter on the bread before adding the filling.
   - Fruity Fusion: Add sliced bananas or strawberries for extra sweetness.
   3. Mascarpone and Berry Alternatives

- Tropical Version: Use mango, pineapple, and passion fruit with coconut cream instead of mascarpone.

- Autumn-Inspired: Swap berries for sliced figs or roasted apples, and drizzle with spiced maple syrup.

Why Sweet Sandwiches Are Irresistible

1. A Perfect Balance of Indulgence and Fun

Sweet sandwiches offer the comfort of traditional desserts with the playful nature of handheld treats.

2. Endless Versatility

From rich, chocolatey creations to light, fruit-forward options, there's a sweet sandwich for every mood and occasion.

3. A Showcase of Creativity

These sandwiches encourage culinary experimentation, allowing you to combine flavors and textures in new and exciting ways.

Crafting Sweet Sandwiches: Final Thoughts

Sweet and dessert sandwiches are a celebration of indulgence, creativity, and fun. Whether you're enjoying the nostalgic charm of an ice cream sandwich, the gooey decadence of a s'mores panini, or the refined elegance of mascarpone and berry toast, these recipes highlight the versatility of dessert sandwiches.

By balancing sweetness, experimenting with textures, and using high-quality ingredients, you can create showstopping sweet sandwiches that delight family, friends, and guests. In the next chapter, we'll explore sandwich accompaniments, from homemade chips to refreshing drinks, to round out your meals perfectly.

Chapter 13: Party Platters and Finger Sandwiches

When it comes to hosting a gathering, nothing delights guests quite like a beautifully arranged platter of finger sandwiches. Perfect for brunches, weddings, baby showers, or casual get-togethers, these bite-sized creations offer elegance, variety, and convenience. From the refreshing simplicity of cucumber sandwiches to the sophistication of smoked salmon canapés and the hearty appeal of mini roast beef sliders, finger sandwiches are versatile enough to suit any occasion.

In this chapter, we'll explore these classic recipes, provide techniques for creating visually appealing platters, and share tips for crafting sandwiches that are as beautiful as they are delicious.

Why Finger Sandwiches Are Perfect for Special Occasions

1. Bite-Sized Elegance

Finger sandwiches are easy to eat, allowing guests to enjoy a variety of flavors without committing to a full sandwich.

Example: Mini roast beef sliders provide a hearty option in a size that won't overwhelm.

2. Versatility

With countless combinations of bread, fillings, and garnishes, finger sandwiches can cater to different tastes, dietary preferences, and themes.

3. Visual Appeal

Arranged thoughtfully, a platter of finger sandwiches becomes a centerpiece that elevates any table setting.

Recipes: Classic Party Sandwiches

1. Cucumber Sandwiches

A quintessential tea-time favorite, cucumber sandwiches are light, refreshing, and simple to prepare. Their delicate flavor makes them a perfect addition to any platter.

Ingredients (Makes 12 sandwiches):

- 6 slices of white or whole-grain bread, crusts removed
- 1/4 cup cream cheese, softened
- 1 tablespoon fresh dill, chopped
- 1 teaspoon lemon juice
- 1/2 cucumber, thinly sliced
- Salt and pepper to taste

Instructions:

1. Prepare the Cream Cheese Spread:
- In a bowl, mix cream cheese, dill, and lemon juice until smooth.
2. Assemble the Sandwiches:
- Spread the cream cheese mixture evenly over each slice of bread.
- Layer cucumber slices on half of the bread slices, slightly overlapping.
- Sprinkle lightly with salt and pepper.
- Top with the remaining slices of bread, cream cheese side down.
3. Slice and Serve:
- Cut each sandwich into quarters or triangles. Arrange neatly on a platter.

Pro Tip: Use a mandoline to slice cucumbers thinly and evenly for a polished look.

2. Smoked Salmon Canapés

These elegant canapés combine the rich flavor of smoked salmon with the tanginess of cream cheese and the brightness of fresh herbs, making them a sophisticated option for any gathering.

Ingredients (Makes 12 canapés):

- 12 small rounds of rye or pumpernickel bread
- 1/4 cup cream cheese, softened
- 1 tablespoon horseradish (optional)
- 6 ounces smoked salmon, thinly sliced
- 1 teaspoon capers

- Fresh dill or chives for garnish

Instructions:

1. Prepare the Bread:

- Cut bread into small rounds using a cookie cutter or knife. Toast lightly if desired.

2. Make the Spread:

- Combine cream cheese and horseradish (if using) in a bowl. Spread a thin layer on each bread round.

3. Assemble the Canapés:

- Top each round with a slice of smoked salmon.

- Garnish with a caper and a sprig of dill or a few chopped chives.

4. Serve: Arrange on a platter and refrigerate until ready to serve.

Pro Tip: Use flavored cream cheese, such as herb or lemon, for an added layer of complexity.

3. Mini Roast Beef Sliders

Hearty and satisfying, these sliders are perfect for adding substance to your sandwich platter. The combination of tender roast beef, tangy horseradish sauce, and soft buns ensures they're a crowd favorite.

Ingredients (Makes 12 sliders):

- 12 slider buns or mini brioche rolls

- 12 slices roast beef (store-bought or homemade)

- 1/4 cup horseradish mayo (mix mayo with a teaspoon of horseradish)

- 12 slices of cheddar or Swiss cheese (optional)

- 12 small leaves of lettuce or arugula

Instructions:

1. Prepare the Buns:

- Slice buns in half and toast lightly if desired.

2. Assemble the Sliders:

- Spread horseradish mayo on the bottom half of each bun.

- Layer a slice of roast beef, cheese (if using), and a leaf of lettuce.

- Close with the top half of the bun.

3. Secure and Serve:

- Use decorative toothpicks to secure each slider. Arrange on a platter.

Pro Tip: Add caramelized onions or a dollop of Dijon mustard for extra flavor.

Creating Visually Appealing Platters

1. Use a Variety of Shapes

Cut sandwiches into different shapes—squares, triangles, or rounds—to add visual interest to your platter.

Example: Pair rectangular cucumber sandwiches with circular smoked salmon canapés.

2. Incorporate Color

Bright garnishes like herbs, edible flowers, and colorful vegetables enhance the visual appeal.

3. Layer Strategically

Arrange sandwiches in overlapping rows or concentric circles for a polished, professional look.

4. Add Decorative Elements

Include non-edible elements like small flags, themed picks, or decorative paper liners to tie the platter into your event's theme.

Tips for Crafting Crowd-Pleasing Finger Sandwiches

1. Prioritize Freshness

Prepare sandwiches close to serving time to ensure bread stays soft and fillings remain fresh.

2. Offer Variety

Provide a mix of flavors and textures—light options like cucumber sandwiches alongside heartier choices like roast beef sliders.

3. Adapt to Dietary Needs

Include vegetarian, vegan, or gluten-free options to accommodate all guests.

4. Keep Them Bite-Sized

Aim for sandwiches that can be eaten in 1-2 bites to make them easy for guests to enjoy without utensils.

Why Finger Sandwiches Shine at Special Occasions

1. Perfect for Mingling

Their portable nature allows guests to enjoy them while socializing, making them ideal for parties and receptions.

2. Elegant and Inviting

A well-crafted platter of finger sandwiches adds a touch of sophistication to any table.

3. Versatile for Any Theme

From casual gatherings to upscale events, finger sandwiches can be tailored to suit any occasion.

Crafting the Ultimate Party Platter: Final Thoughts

Finger sandwiches and party platters are more than just appetizers—they're an opportunity to showcase your creativity and hospitality. Whether you're offering the refreshing crunch of cucumber sandwiches, the refined flavors of smoked salmon canapés, or the hearty appeal of mini roast beef sliders, these recipes and tips will help you create a spread that impresses and delights.

By focusing on fresh ingredients, thoughtful presentation, and a mix of flavors, you can craft platters that become the highlight of any event. In the next chapter, we'll explore breakfast and brunch sandwich options, perfect for starting your day or hosting a mid-morning gathering.

Chapter 14: Picnic and Outdoor Sandwiches

Picnic and outdoor sandwiches are a cornerstone of casual gatherings, providing a convenient, portable, and satisfying meal that can be enjoyed in the fresh air. Whether you're planning a family picnic, a day at the park, or a beach outing, the right sandwich can elevate your outdoor dining experience. Recipes like the muffuletta, Italian sub, and chicken Caesar wrap are not only flavorful but also built to travel well, making them perfect for al fresco dining.

In this chapter, we'll dive into these iconic recipes, explore tips for keeping sandwiches fresh and portable, and share ideas for creating the ultimate outdoor sandwich experience.

Why Sandwiches Are Perfect for Picnics and Outdoor Dining

1. Portable and Convenient

Sandwiches are inherently easy to transport and eat without utensils, making them ideal for outdoor settings.

Example: The muffuletta's pressed layers stay intact even during travel, ensuring a mess-free meal.

2. Endless Variety

With countless combinations of bread, fillings, and spreads, sandwiches cater to every taste and dietary preference.

3. Easy to Prepare Ahead

Many picnic sandwiches can be made in advance, allowing flavors to meld and making day-of preparation a breeze.

Recipes: Picnic and Outdoor Sandwich Favorites

1. Muffuletta

Originating in New Orleans, the muffuletta is a hearty sandwich layered with Italian meats, cheeses, and a zesty olive salad, all pressed between a large round loaf. Its sturdy structure makes it perfect for travel.

Ingredients (Serves 4-6):
- 1 round loaf of Italian or sesame bread
- 1/2 cup olive salad (recipe below)
- 4 ounces salami, thinly sliced
- 4 ounces mortadella or ham, thinly sliced
- 4 ounces provolone cheese, thinly sliced
- 4 ounces mozzarella cheese, thinly sliced

For Olive Salad:
- 1/2 cup chopped green olives
- 1/4 cup chopped black olives
- 1/4 cup roasted red peppers, diced
- 1 tablespoon capers
- 2 tablespoons olive oil
- 1 tablespoon red wine vinegar
- 1 teaspoon minced garlic
- 1 teaspoon dried oregano

Instructions:

1. Make the Olive Salad: Combine all olive salad ingredients in a bowl and let marinate for at least 30 minutes.

2. Prepare the Bread: Slice the loaf in half horizontally and hollow out some of the bread from the top and bottom halves.

3. Assemble the Sandwich:
- Spread half the olive salad on the bottom half of the bread.
- Layer salami, mortadella, provolone, mozzarella, and the remaining olive salad.
- Close with the top half of the bread and press down firmly.

4. Wrap and Press: Wrap the sandwich tightly in plastic wrap or foil. Place in the refrigerator with a heavy object on top to press it for at least 2 hours or overnight.

5. Serve: Slice into wedges or squares for easy serving.

Pro Tip: Muffulettas taste even better when made a day ahead, allowing the flavors to meld.

2. Italian Sub

The Italian sub is a deli classic, featuring layers of cured meats, cheeses, and vegetables dressed with tangy vinaigrette, all served on a long, crusty roll.

Ingredients (Serves 2-4):

- 1 large Italian hoagie roll or baguette
- 4 ounces salami, thinly sliced
- 4 ounces capicola or ham, thinly sliced
- 4 ounces provolone cheese, thinly sliced
- 1/4 cup shredded lettuce
- 1/4 cup sliced tomatoes
- 1/4 cup sliced red onions
- 1/4 cup sliced banana peppers (optional)
- 2 tablespoons olive oil
- 1 tablespoon red wine vinegar
- 1 teaspoon dried oregano
- Salt and pepper to taste

Instructions:

1. Prepare the Roll: Slice the roll in half lengthwise and hollow out some of the interior to make room for the fillings.

2. Layer the Ingredients:

- Drizzle olive oil and red wine vinegar on both halves of the bread.

- Layer salami, capicola, provolone, lettuce, tomatoes, onions, and banana peppers.

- Sprinkle with oregano, salt, and pepper.

3. Close and Secure: Close the sandwich and wrap tightly in parchment paper or foil.

4. Serve: Slice into portions and serve immediately or pack for travel.

Pro Tip: Add a smear of pesto or a drizzle of balsamic glaze for a gourmet twist.

3. Chicken Caesar Wrap

This modern wrap combines the flavors of a classic Caesar salad with tender chicken, crisp romaine, and tangy dressing, all wrapped in a soft tortilla for easy portability.

Ingredients (Serves 2):
- 2 large flour tortillas
- 2 cups cooked, shredded chicken (rotisserie or grilled)
- 2 cups chopped romaine lettuce
- 1/4 cup Caesar dressing (homemade or store-bought)
- 1/4 cup grated Parmesan cheese
- 1/4 cup croutons, crushed
- Optional: sliced avocado or cherry tomatoes

Instructions:

1. Prepare the Filling: In a bowl, toss chicken, romaine, Caesar dressing, Parmesan, and crushed croutons until evenly coated.

2. Assemble the Wraps:
- Lay a tortilla flat and place half the filling in the center.
- Add optional toppings like avocado or cherry tomatoes.
- Fold in the sides and roll tightly from the bottom up.

3. Wrap and Pack: Wrap each tortilla in parchment paper or foil to secure it.

4. Serve: Slice in half and enjoy immediately or pack for travel.

Pro Tip: For a lighter version, use whole-grain tortillas and Greek yogurt-based Caesar dressing.

Tips for Packing Sandwiches to Stay Fresh and Portable

1. Choose the Right Bread

Opt for sturdy bread like baguettes, ciabatta, or tortillas that can withstand moisture without becoming soggy.

2. Layer Thoughtfully

- Place wetter ingredients like tomatoes or dressings in the center of the sandwich, away from the bread.

- Use a barrier layer like lettuce, cheese, or cured meats to protect the bread from moisture.

3. Wrap Securely

Wrap sandwiches tightly in parchment paper, foil, or reusable wraps to keep them intact and easy to handle.

4. Keep Cool

Use an insulated cooler or ice packs to maintain freshness, especially for sandwiches with perishable ingredients like meats or mayonnaise-based dressings.

5. Pack Condiments Separately

For sandwiches that include spreads or dressings, consider packing them separately and adding them just before eating to prevent sogginess.

Enhancing Your Outdoor Sandwich Experience

1. Include Side Dishes

Pair sandwiches with portable sides like fresh fruit, potato chips, or pasta salads for a complete meal.

2. Add Drinks

Bring along refreshing beverages like lemonade, iced tea, or sparkling water to complement your meal.

3. Create a Picnic-Friendly Presentation

Use reusable containers, cutting boards, and serving utensils to create a stylish and eco-friendly setup.

4. Think About Clean-Up

Pack napkins, wet wipes, and trash bags to make post-picnic cleanup easy and hassle-free.

Why Picnic Sandwiches Are a Must-Have

Picnic and outdoor sandwiches strike the perfect balance between practicality and deliciousness. They're easy to prepare, travel well, and offer endless customization options. Whether it's the robust flavors of a muffuletta, the tangy layers of an Italian sub, or the fresh, handheld convenience of a chicken Caesar wrap, these sandwiches ensure your outdoor dining experience is both satisfying and stress-free.

By following thoughtful packing techniques and incorporating complementary sides and drinks, you can elevate any picnic into a memorable event. In the next chapter, we'll explore how to pair sandwiches with drinks, sides, and desserts for a complete and harmonious meal experience.

Chapter 15: Seasonal Sandwiches

Sandwiches are a culinary canvas that can beautifully reflect the flavors of each season. Whether you're savoring the warmth of a Thanksgiving leftover sandwich in winter, the bright freshness of a summer tomato and basil sandwich, or the cozy indulgence of a fall harvest grilled cheese, seasonal sandwiches celebrate the best ingredients each time of year has to offer. By using locally sourced, in-season produce and complementary flavors, you can elevate a simple sandwich into a memorable meal.

In this chapter, we'll explore these three recipes, discuss how to incorporate seasonal ingredients into your sandwiches, and provide tips for creating unique, seasonal variations throughout the year.

Why Seasonal Sandwiches Are Special

1. Highlighting Peak Flavors
Using seasonal ingredients ensures that your sandwiches are made with produce at its freshest and most flavorful.
Example: A summer tomato and basil sandwich captures the vibrant, juicy essence of sun-ripened tomatoes.
2. Supporting Local and Sustainable Eating
Seasonal ingredients are often locally grown, reducing their environmental impact while supporting local farmers.
3. Embracing Creativity
Seasonal sandwiches inspire you to experiment with new flavors, textures, and combinations based on what's available.

Recipes: Seasonal Sandwich Favorites

1. Thanksgiving Leftover Sandwich

A Thanksgiving leftover sandwich is the perfect way to repurpose holiday meals into a satisfying, flavor-packed creation. Layers of turkey, stuffing, cranberry sauce, and gravy come together in this indulgent sandwich.

Ingredients (Serves 2):

- 4 slices of sturdy bread (sourdough or multigrain)
- 6 ounces cooked turkey, sliced
- 1/2 cup stuffing or dressing
- 1/4 cup cranberry sauce
- 1/4 cup gravy (optional, for dipping)
- 2 tablespoons mayonnaise or butter

Instructions:

1. Prepare the Bread: Toast the bread lightly for added structure. Spread mayonnaise or butter on one side of each slice.

2. Layer the Ingredients:

- On the bottom slice, layer turkey, stuffing, and cranberry sauce.
- Add a second slice of bread to close the sandwich.

3. Optional Warm-Up: If desired, grill the sandwich lightly in a skillet to warm the fillings and crisp the bread.

4. Serve: Slice in half and serve with a side of warm gravy for dipping.

Pro Tip: Add leftover roasted vegetables or mashed potatoes for extra layers of flavor.

2. Summer Tomato and Basil Sandwich

This light and refreshing sandwich is a tribute to the vibrant flavors of summer. Juicy tomatoes, fragrant basil, and creamy mozzarella are layered on crusty bread, making for a simple yet delicious meal.

Ingredients (Serves 2):

- 1 baguette or ciabatta loaf
- 2 large ripe tomatoes, sliced

- 4 ounces fresh mozzarella, sliced
- 8-10 fresh basil leaves
- 2 tablespoons extra-virgin olive oil
- 1 tablespoon balsamic glaze
- Salt and black pepper to taste

Instructions:

1. Prepare the Bread: Slice the baguette or ciabatta in half lengthwise and toast lightly.

2. Assemble the Sandwich:

- Drizzle olive oil on both halves of the bread.
- Layer tomato slices, mozzarella, and basil leaves.
- Drizzle with balsamic glaze and season with salt and pepper.

3. Close and Serve: Close the sandwich, slice into portions, and enjoy immediately.

Pro Tip: Add avocado or a smear of pesto for a richer flavor.

3. Fall Harvest Grilled Cheese

This autumn-inspired grilled cheese combines earthy roasted vegetables, sharp cheddar, and a hint of sweetness from apple slices, creating a cozy, comforting sandwich.

Ingredients (Serves 2):

- 4 slices of multigrain or sourdough bread
- 1 cup roasted butternut squash or sweet potatoes, mashed
- 1/2 apple, thinly sliced
- 4 ounces sharp cheddar cheese, sliced
- 2 tablespoons butter

Instructions:

1. Prepare the Bread: Spread butter on one side of each slice of bread.

2. Assemble the Sandwich:

- On the unbuttered side of two slices, spread a layer of mashed squash or sweet potatoes.
- Add apple slices and cheddar cheese.
- Close with the remaining slices of bread, buttered side out.

3. Grill the Sandwich: Heat a skillet over medium heat and grill the sandwiches until golden brown on both sides and the cheese is melted, about 3-4 minutes per side.

4. Serve: Slice and enjoy warm.

Pro Tip: Add caramelized onions or a sprinkle of cinnamon for extra depth.

Incorporating Seasonal Ingredients

1. Understanding Seasonal Availability

Choose ingredients that are at their peak during each season:

- Spring: Asparagus, peas, radishes, fresh herbs.
- Summer: Tomatoes, cucumbers, basil, corn.
- Fall: Squash, apples, mushrooms, kale.
- Winter: Root vegetables, citrus, hearty greens.

2. Pairing Flavors Thoughtfully

Combine complementary flavors to enhance the seasonal theme:

- Example: Pair tart cranberries with savory turkey in a winter sandwich.

3. Experimenting with Local Ingredients

Visit farmers' markets to discover unique, local produce that can inspire creative sandwich combinations.

Tips for Crafting Seasonal Sandwiches

1. Prioritize Freshness

Use the freshest ingredients available to maximize flavor and texture.

2. Balance Flavors and Textures

Create a balance of sweet, savory, creamy, and crunchy elements:

- Example: Add crisp apple slices to a creamy grilled cheese for contrast.

3. Adjust for Dietary Preferences

Customize sandwiches with plant-based, gluten-free, or dairy-free options to cater to dietary needs.

4. Keep It Simple

Let the seasonal ingredients shine by using minimal seasoning and preparation.

Why Seasonal Sandwiches Are Irresistible

1. A Celebration of Nature's Bounty

Seasonal sandwiches capture the essence of each season, offering a fresh and flavorful way to enjoy nature's best.

2. A Versatile Meal Option

These sandwiches can be served as casual meals, elegant appetizers, or picnic staples.

3. A Source of Inspiration

By exploring seasonal ingredients, you can discover new flavor combinations and techniques to enhance your sandwich-making skills.

Final Thoughts: Seasonal Sandwich Creativity

Seasonal sandwiches are more than just meals—they're a celebration of the changing seasons and the vibrant ingredients they bring. Whether you're indulging in the comforting layers of a Thanksgiving leftover sandwich, savoring the fresh simplicity of a summer tomato and basil creation, or cozying up with a fall harvest grilled cheese, these recipes showcase the potential of seasonal eating.

By embracing the best ingredients each season has to offer and experimenting with flavors, you can create sandwiches that are not only delicious but also a true reflection of the time of year. As we conclude this exploration of sandwiches, remember that the possibilities are endless—every ingredient, season, and occasion presents a new opportunity to craft something truly special.

Conclusion: Your Sandwich Journey

The sandwich is far more than just a convenient meal—it's a blank canvas for culinary creativity, a symbol of connection, and a gateway to exploring global flavors. As you've journeyed through the chapters of this book, you've discovered the versatility of sandwiches, from classic comfort food to gourmet creations, and from simple breakfast fare to extravagant party platters.

In this final chapter, we'll reflect on the role sandwiches play in bringing people together, encourage you to experiment and create your own signature sandwiches, and share essential tips for perfecting the art of sandwich-making.

The Sandwich as a Universal Comfort

1. A Culinary Common Ground

Sandwiches transcend cultures and cuisines, serving as a universal symbol of comfort and satisfaction.

- Example: A bánh mì reflects the flavors of Vietnam, while an Italian sub embodies Mediterranean influences.

- Why it Matters: Sandwiches bridge cultural divides, offering a familiar format with endless variations that cater to personal tastes and traditions.

2. A Meal for Every Occasion

From quick lunches to elegant gatherings, sandwiches adapt effortlessly to any setting.

- Casual Comfort: A peanut butter and jelly sandwich evokes childhood nostalgia.

- Sophisticated Elegance: A smoked salmon canapé elevates a dinner party.

3. Bringing People Together

Sharing a platter of sandwiches at a picnic, a party, or a family dinner fosters connection and camaraderie.

- Why It Works: The simplicity of sandwiches allows people to focus on the experience rather than the meal's complexity, making them perfect for communal dining.

Encouragement to Experiment

1. Think Beyond the Basics

Don't be afraid to push the boundaries of traditional sandwich-making. Experiment with unique ingredients, textures, and techniques.

- Example: Try incorporating global flavors, such as harissa-spiced vegetables, or experiment with unconventional bases like waffles or lettuce wraps.

2. Create Your Own Signature Sandwich

Use your favorite ingredients to craft a sandwich that represents your taste and creativity.

- Tips for Personalization:
- Choose a base: Select a bread or wrap that complements your ingredients.
- Layer flavors: Balance sweet, savory, tangy, and spicy elements.
- Add texture: Incorporate both crunchy and creamy components.
- Finish with flair: Use sauces, drizzles, or garnishes to make it memorable.

3. Let the Seasons Inspire You

Take cues from the seasons to craft sandwiches that highlight fresh, in-season ingredients.

- Example: A summer tomato and basil sandwich celebrates the peak of tomato season, while a winter sandwich might feature roasted root vegetables and melted Gruyère.

The Role of Sandwiches in Bringing People Together

1. A Food of Inclusion

Sandwiches can be customized to cater to different dietary preferences, ensuring everyone feels included.

- Example: A sandwich platter can feature vegetarian, vegan, gluten-free, and meat-based options, allowing guests to choose what suits them best.

2. A Catalyst for Conversation

Sandwiches often spark discussions about culture, creativity, and personal preferences, deepening connections around the table.

- Example: Sharing stories about family recipes, like a favorite Thanksgiving leftover sandwich, fosters a sense of community.

3. A Shared Experience

Whether enjoying a casual picnic or a gourmet sandwich meal, sandwiches create shared memories that last long after the meal is over.

Final Tips for Perfecting the Art of Sandwich-Making

1. Balance Flavors Thoughtfully

Every great sandwich strikes a balance between flavors:

- Sweet and savory (e.g., honey-glazed ham with sharp cheddar).
- Tangy and creamy (e.g., pickles with aioli).
- Spicy and mild (e.g., jalapeños with creamy avocado).

2. Prioritize Quality Ingredients

The success of a sandwich often lies in the quality of its components.

- Bread: Use fresh, high-quality bread as the foundation.
- Proteins: Choose flavorful meats, cheeses, or plant-based alternatives.
- Produce: Opt for fresh, in-season vegetables and fruits.
- Spreads: Experiment with homemade spreads like aioli, pestos, or flavored butters.

3. Play with Textures

Incorporate contrasting textures for a dynamic eating experience:

- Crunchy elements: Toasted bread, nuts, or crispy lettuce.
- Creamy components: Cheese, avocado, or hummus.
- Chewy or tender fillings: Meats, roasted vegetables, or mushrooms.

4. Master the Assembly

How you layer your ingredients matters.

- Pro Tip: Place wetter ingredients, like tomatoes or sauces, in the middle to avoid soggy bread.
- Visual Appeal: Layer ingredients thoughtfully for a colorful, Instagram-worthy presentation.

5. Embrace Simplicity

Some of the best sandwiches are the simplest. Focus on a few high-quality ingredients rather than overloading with too many elements.

6. Practice Presentation

A well-plated sandwich is more inviting.

- Slice sandwiches cleanly with a sharp knife.

- Arrange platters with variety in shapes and sizes for visual interest.

- Use garnishes like herbs, edible flowers, or a drizzle of sauce for a polished look.

Reflecting on Your Sandwich Journey

1. The Joy of Discovery

Through this book, you've explored the versatility of sandwiches, from global flavors to sweet indulgences, and from gourmet creations to casual staples. Each recipe and tip has aimed to inspire you to experiment and elevate your sandwich-making skills.

2. The Endless Possibilities

The beauty of sandwiches lies in their infinite potential for innovation. With countless combinations of ingredients and techniques, the possibilities are limited only by your imagination.

3. A Timeless Classic

As much as sandwiches evolve, their core appeal remains unchanged: they're simple, satisfying, and universally loved.

Final Thoughts: Crafting Your Legacy

Your sandwich journey doesn't end here. With the knowledge, inspiration, and confidence gained from this book, you're equipped to create sandwiches that reflect your personality, honor traditions, and push culinary boundaries. Whether you're preparing a quick lunch, hosting a lavish party, or crafting a meal for a loved one, your sandwiches have the power to bring joy, connection, and creativity to the table.

So go forth, experiment, and let your sandwiches tell your story. The world of sandwiches is yours to explore—one delicious bite at a time.

Don't miss out!

Visit the website below and you can sign up to receive emails whenever Olivia Bennett publishes a new book. There's no charge and no obligation.

https://books2read.com/r/B-A-QLEKD-NQIAG

BOOKS2READ

Connecting independent readers to independent writers.

About the Author

Olivia Bennett is a celebrated food writer and chef with expertise spanning multiple culinary disciplines. With a passion for making home cooking accessible, she specializes in guiding readers through everything from hearty casseroles to delicate pastries. Her work is known for its clear instructions, practical tips, and deep understanding of both traditional and modern cooking techniques.